DIS-
ORGA-
NISA-
TION
&
SEX

Jamieson Webster

DIS-
ORGA-
NISA-
TION
&
SEX

DIVIDED

Published in the United Kingdom by Divided in 2022.

Divided Publishing
251 Avenue Louise, 2nd floor
1050 Brussels
Belgium

https://divided.online

Printed by Graphius Brussels

ISBN 978-1-9164250-9-5

it ends when I go to sleep

Part 4
Sex Life

Preface

When I think about sex as psychoanalysis conceives of it, I hear the phrase 'Water, water everywhere, nor any drop to drink' from Coleridge's *Rime of the Ancient Mariner*. Granted this is a particularly hysterical way of parsing a problem replete with voracious orality, an emphasis on dissatisfaction, and a metaphoric density bordering on confusion, but why not begin with a confession of my oral issues? It's impetuous, and it knows no bounds – I simply love the pleasures of the mouth. I'm telling you it's a sexual desert out there, while speaking to the reality of sexual fluids, and a desire for fluid-like sexual exchange. I'm telling you my concerns about a kind of contemporary sexual anorexia or sexual dehydration. Sex is sometimes felt as a curse and not a cure, though for the ancient mariner the cure was to learn to love the albatross, not to fear it. To this end, I want to speak to the importance of sex and the rarity of sex in the psychoanalytic sense; the extreme search one has to engage in to find what can assuage a thirst. Sex has the power to bring something revelatory, a satisfaction that we name sexual which *changes something in reality*. At my most open, I want us to all be on this adventure.

For psychoanalysis, sex and civilisation are in a tight dialectical relationship: human sexuality is unnatural, meaning it goes beyond the programme that can define life. Sex needs life to create forms that can meet its anarchic, unquenchable nature. Sex presses us up against the ways we attempt to organise its excess. Sex disorganises. What might contain it? Whatever our solutions or satisfactions, from artistic expressions to scientific inventions, the multitude of institutions centred on the body, on education, on consumerism and the family, these are always, only, partial solutions – for a time, for one singular individual, for one specific societal locale. If we start to fear that we cannot offer adequate containment, we can initiate attempts to bring desire under wraps and at our most violent, kill it, desiccate the environs, even at our own cost. This desire and its impediments, civilisation and its discontents, defines what psychoanalysis understands about human life as sex life.

I am reminded of my water breaking – I recently had a daughter – and the panic it induced in the medical personnel who need the breaking of waters to line up seamlessly with readiness to give birth; it often does not. So they force the issue and it is unpleasant; a series of painful interventions that make you wonder who invented them and whether it was with the actual body with sexual organs in mind. As a psychoanalyst, in my experience, the strangest and cruellest practices are driven from the places where medical attention to the body and the question of sex are close. You get a feeling that the sexuality of bodies brings medical practitioners towards something they don't understand, perhaps don't want to understand, and need to feel is separate from the work that they do.

Sex in psychoanalysis at its most clichéd often brings up the trope of a desire to return to the womb, reverse-birth as a return to the water, to the safe environs of the motherland. But the psychoanalytic message emphasises the barriers to this fantasy. We humans cannot return to the womb because billions of years ago we crawled from the seas onto land. Our time in amniotic fluids isn't even a memory, even when it is a reality, even when it is our point of origin, now only existing in the form of a desire that is forced to search for it knows not what. The ice age for Freud, when the seas dried up or froze, is the mythic moment of the birth of neurotic sexuality. Human sexuality stranded on land. The project is the pursuit of a more fluid sexuality. This is the question of sex in psychoanalysis as I understand it.

My previous book had 'disorder' in the title; this became an important word for me, a way to resist the psychiatric love of multiplying the realm of supposed disorders, especially personality disorders. I embraced disorder in the book; I don't know what a personality is. In this newly edited collection of papers, 'disorganisation' speaks to an illusion about organisation. Sometimes I like to think this illusion is beginning to evaporate. During my clinical training, 'disorganised' was a word we used psychiatrically to label someone's thoughts that were seen as scattered, fragmented, splintering, that couldn't be gathered and made coherent. But who could be the judge of what counted as coherent? Did we really believe that there was such an ideal person? While the previous book links the body to disorder, this one links sex to disorganisation. We encounter an everyday demand to put our bodies and our ideas in some kind of order, to streamline our sex life, to reproduce the image of 'settling down'. Psychoanalysis says, point blank, that nothing could be more impossible, and nothing is more counterproductive to the sexuality unique to human beings; one that, as Freud points out, goes beyond instinct, beyond pleasure, and is thus radically open. Open, but for carrying the burden of history.

In a book about sex, I decided to shift to a word that has 'organ' in it – importantly, in the form of its undoing. Lacan remarked that post-coitus our organs are sidelined: we are stripped of them, uncocked, as intensity leaves our body. Perhaps this is the point of orgasm – taking us (our wishes and expectations) down a notch, leaving us with nothing but scattered memories and traces of excitement and tenderness, grasping at these after-pleasures. These pieces of sex life are what we have, a minimal organisation, a kind of disorganised amalgam, and a precious one. I recently encountered Oliver Davis and Tim Dean's book *Hatred of Sex* (University of Nebraska Press, 2022), which opens with this polemical provocation: 'Like democracy, sex is messy and disordering, hateable as well as desireable.' The question is how to welcome the disorder and the disorganising force of sex (and democracy), and the ways that resistance to it, and indeed hatred of it, are being utilised for the purposes of anti-democratic power. This is the contemporary crisis the authors see in rising autocracies, and no less in multiplying conspiracies, like QAnon. These organs of organisation. Here Davis and Dean contextualise the term 'hatred': 'Sex betokens . . . the highly complex relationship that all humans have with their body's capacity for intense, even excessive pleasure. It is the underestimated difficulty of that relationship with one's own pleasures that prompts us to speak in terms of a distinct hatred of sex.'

A question of the psychoanalytic cure that touches psychoanalysis with respect to its knowledge, its institutes and the passing down of clinical knowledge: what organisation is possible that allows for the place of disorganisation, messiness, difficulty? The story of psychoanalytic institutes and psychoanalytic training does not fare well in this arena; there is calcification of sexuality in these institutional forms and bureaucratic regulations. Freud had the audacity to imagine a civilisation that could tolerate the sheer multiplicity of sexuality, the singularity of individual styles of pleasure and unpleasure, of which the psychoanalyst has the odd glimpse in clinical work. The psychoanalyst is the one who takes on the burden of disorganisation and tries, at all costs, to do something other than make it go away. We do so with no guarantee and at great risk. We do so having to test everything on ourselves first, knowing that where we falter, step back, we will never be able to lead our patients all that much further. Can't you almost envision a form of democracy that takes on this manner, this same weight of responsibility? Water, everywhere.

Just this evening my daughter and I were playing at taking turns sucking on each other's faces, my chin, her mouth, my cheek, her neck. The pleasure was ecstatic, not just because of the pleasure of sucking, the pleasure of the lips and the tongue, but also the game of it, the furtive exchange of gazes, the unfolding and developing rhythms, the play of choice around where, when, how hard, and always a question of when to stop. It was late. She soon grew tired. When infants are sleepy they are more disorganised; like loose ends, their bodies fray around the edges and they are unsure of what to do with themselves. Sometimes her knees buckle out from under her. Many times she does something very special at this place of disorganisation, which I've come to marvel at: she invents something new as a way of soothing herself, extending pleasure, and falling asleep (no doubt entering that miraculous space of disorganisation known as dream life). It's a little like why we have our patients lie down on a couch – to get closer to this. Tonight, she figured out that not only could she suck, she could blow, and she could make the most incredible noises, which created a whole song that made me laugh and laugh and laugh, which pleased her, but not any more than she had already pleased herself. I know because once I was quiet, she continued as if I wasn't there, refining her instrument, playing with her new organ, until she slept.

Part 1

Unconscious Truth, Sexuality, Act

The Disorganising Force of Desire

1. Lacan's anti-progressivism

Time, despite its obvious regularity, has an evanescent and capricious character. Time as catastrophic, for example, or time as paradise regained, is a timeless time or a time that seems to break out of time. There is also the feeling of being stuck in time – the time of stasis, of waiting, of anxious apprehension. These times are burdened by the sensation of their being too thick or too thin, too concrete or too excitable. Procrastination, ennui, languor, anticipation, impatience, all come to mind. Are these not an attempt to fix time, to *apprehend* time, here in both meanings of the word – to arrest, and to understand? The attempt to say, *I am here and that will (or will not) be there*, gives a feeling of time as a linear construction. You can place yourself on a point on a line. Even in catastrophic time, for example, you have the sense of a line culminating at an endpoint.

Jacques Lacan, while recognising this phenomenology of time – particularly in relation to neurosis and psychoanalytic treatment – emphasised the imaginary aspects of this way of thinking. For example, what is operative is often something like the projection of wish. The oceanic feeling, as Sigmund Freud points out, is the wish for a return to the protection of omnipotent parental love and the attempt to experience a kind of boundless narcissism.[1] Procrastination, Lacan points out, is a kind of anal relationship to time, by which omnipotence is retained through a refusal of time. There is also a time that stands in opposition to these more 'imaginary' times. This time is closer to a conception of time that is rhythmic rather than linear; a time that stresses return, repetition, breaks, openings and closings, and not endless progression or progression to an end. It is closer to the movements of unconscious desire and the different order of time that Freud marked when writing about the unconscious.

Lacan emphasises the importance of a differentiation in these registers of time, particularly when reflecting on the moment when psychoanalysis comes into being. He reminds us that the turn of the century was a juncture of history when the idea of 'progress' was slowly becoming the dominant model. Progress is a new concept – not more than one hundred years old – tied to the modern subject of science. There is an illusion of timelessness that the idea of progress gives off despite this rather recent birthright, and psychoanalysis, he felt, was a challenge to this linear ordering.

How can we think of anything without thinking of progress? On first reflection, it seems almost impossible. Progress appears as an incontestable good. One *must* progress. What else is there? Progress sets an intrinsic value on human civilisation. One should remember Freud's cautious final remarks in *Civilization and Its Discontents* (1930):

> It is very far from my intention to express an opinion upon the value of human civilization. I have endeavoured to guard myself against the enthusiastic prejudice which holds that our civilization is the most precious thing we possess or could acquire and that its path will necessarily lead to heights of unimaginable perfection . . . One thing only do I know for certain and that is that man's judgments of value follow directly his wish for happiness – that, accordingly, they are an attempt to support his illusions with arguments.[2]

For Lacan, the conceit of an unquestionable value placed on the present of civilisation could not be the 'world-view' of psychoanalysis.

History in the psychoanalytic vein of thought is neither linear, nor modelled on the approach to perfection, nor bound up with mastery or fulfilment. History for psychoanalysis happens in fits and starts, in a series of formative crises and their resolution, 'in breaks, in a succession of trials and openings that have at every stage deluded us into thinking that we could launch into a totality'.[3] History is a drawn-out confrontation between man and his illusions, disappointments, and an impossible relation to satisfaction. In this sense time is much more circular and, indeed, regressive. Seeing things this way, however pessimistically, Lacan sees as an ethical standpoint inherent to Freud's project:

> Whether people are civilized or not, enlightened or not, they are capable of the same collective enthusiasms, the same passions. They are always at a level that there is no reason to describe as higher or lower, as affective, passionate, or supposedly intellectual, or developed, as they say. The same choices are available to all of them, and they can translate into the same successes or the same aberrations. This message that Freud brings is definitely not discordant with what has happened since his day, and that should inspire us to take a much more modest view of the possibility of progress in thought. Anyone who takes the trouble to try to get back to the level where this message has some effect is sure to be closer to what is singular in psychoanalysis.[4]

The ideal of progress forces one to try and anxiously hold the future captive, which runs the risk of abandoning a modesty singular to psychoanalysis.

2. Desire is oriented towards, but not on, the future

What is singular in psychoanalysis for Lacan is the discovery of the unconscious, and, in particular, the discovery of unconscious desire. While Lacan has popularised the idea of desire, what is so fascinating and distinct about this category is easily lost, much, I suppose, like desire itself. Abiding by the old Freudian opposition between ego-libido and object-libido, narcissism and desire, death drive and life drive, Lacan's claim is that what psychoanalysis does is 'give us back our desire'. Furthermore, this desire is oriented towards, but not on, the future.

It is important to understand that for Lacan desire cannot be taken on the model of a biological need or a conscious wish, as in the wish for a new car or a girlfriend or a bagel. To say that desire is unconscious, tied into an unconscious network of wishes, is a starting point. If I say, *I wish you would love me, I wish you would see me, I wish I could take possession of you*, here we are a little closer to what Lacan is talking about. When I say, *I love you*, or *I wish you would love me*, rather than any of these statements being some kind of incarnation, as in an end-expressionist theory of desire, they are only the beginning. *Love me how? See me in what way? Possession? Really? What did you have in mind?*

What this brings to bear is not the satisfaction of desire, but its impossible, never total, only partial satisfaction, the pursuit of which creates our subjectivity and our world. What Lacan will stress is that this involves neither the adaptation of desire to the world (a kind of taming of it), nor of the world to our desire (a kind of domination of the outside), but an alignment of the subject with their unknown desire. Desire, Lacan says, is 'in you more than you'.[5]

Likewise, the psychoanalyst in the consulting room abides by this model – think of what happens when a patient wants to logically progress in a session with their thoughts. Never to us, strangely, do they sound worse. The reason? It is a strategy to avoid unconscious desire. As Philip Rieff puts it: if the demands of efficiency in the modern world turn all time into money, psychoanalysis does the reverse, elevating inefficiency and turning money back into time.[6] If our future is increasingly hemmed in by the demands of contemporary life, psychoanalysis demands that it re-open, even if only in the space of an hour.

This fundamental break that psychoanalysis creates is always, for Lacan, related to what is radical and nuanced about this category of the sexual in the unconscious. The movements of desire displace an implicit trend towards mastery, totality, unification and essentialism; and so desire continues to be an open site of investigation and possibility. Or, to put it more strongly: sexual desire is the open site *par excellence*.

From a selective angle, Lacan emphasises desire, not the object which may attempt to satisfy it or not. In any case, in Freud's *Three Essays on the Theory of Sexuality* (1905), the object of the sexual drive was its most variable aspect – it could be anything, a person, a feeling, a hand, a shoe.[7] The anti-progressive Lacan meets with an anti-utilitarian understanding of desire – the more impossible the desire, the stronger it is. Pathology then is emphasised *only* in light of the varied failures of libido, its withdrawal and stagnation inward – what used to be implied by the narcissistic neuroses or fixation, for example, and not by the realistic and satisfactory deployment of desire as such.

There is an emphasis on movement, time, as tied to desire, and their relation to the question of the future of psychoanalysis seems inextricably linked. The gift of time in psychoanalysis is also the gift of desire, and psychoanalysis seems to have lost sight of this gift in an anxiety that runs counter to its offer. Perhaps in getting closer to desire, we may free psychoanalysis from what has come to feel like its loudly ticking clock.

So the questions concern the telos of psychoanalysis, the future of psychoanalysis not as a question of ends, as in means to an end, or progress to the end – as the point where it either dies, realises itself, or knows itself in full – but as its *raison d'être*. In other words, the message psychoanalysis has with respect to *desire*. What psychoanalysis can demonstrate is how, with great difficulty, desire brings about new ways of living with unconscious desire and sexuality, how symptoms can inform a mode of passionate subjectivity. For myself, I would like to pare down progress, the conception of the future organisation of our field, to the disorganising force of these lines of desire.

3. A young Freud on the future of psychoanalysis

One of the less touted components of Lacan's teaching was aimed at separating this truth that emerged, the discovery of psychoanalysis, from the unavoidable phantasmatic or imaginary portion of Freud's desire. I will engage in just such an analysis by turning to a few papers by Freud where he discusses the progress and future of psychoanalytic knowledge, in particular his early paper of 1910, 'The Future Prospects of Psycho-Analytic Therapy', and his 1919 paper 'Lines of Advance in Psycho-Analytic Therapy'. The two papers couldn't express more antithetical views on the prospects of this strange discipline, one seeing the field of psychoanalysis as more and more organised, institutionalised and authoritative, with the other finding any such programme impossible given the nature of the discipline. If we see Freud finally giving up on a question of the future, what does this mean, and why is it still a question so many others continue to linger on?

A young and zealous Freud addresses the Second Psycho-Analytical Congress in 1910 on 'The Future Prospects of Psycho-Analytic Therapy'. He would like the audience to know, straight off, that 'we have by no means come to the *end* of our resources for combating the neuroses'.[8] One can't help but notice an anxiety concerning 'ends' arising before he's even begun. He continues, 'reinforcement will come . . . from three directions: 1) From Internal Progress 2) From Increased Authority and 3) From the General Effect of our Work'.[9] With respect to the first direction, internal progress, Freud means to address analytic knowledge and technique. The assistance of the analyst, he says, has become clear: we plant a seed and wait for it to come to fruition, what he calls a conscious anticipatory idea, given by the analyst, which the patient can then find in himself, and the analyst can await confirmation. You can imagine this little game of anticipating future certainty. We already know that Freud never went on to write the definitive work on technique, *The General Methodology of Psycho-Analysis*. At the very least this abandoned project poses questions about this articulation of internal progress.

Freud continues. He says he 'hopes' that the audience will form an impression 'that when we know all that we now only suspect and when we have carried out all the improvements in technique to which deeper observation of our patients is bound to lead us, our medical procedure will reach a degree of precision and certainty of success'.[10] Success that he models after the 'obstetrician' who need only examine a 'placenta to know whether it has been completely expelled or whether noxious fragments of it still remain'.[11] Like the obstetrician, the analyst shall be able to know whether his work has been 'definitively successful'. Thus ends his first future prospect.

It's not the naivety of Freud that I'd like to point out here (I find it quite charming really), but this dream of progress. Here, with Freud, we encounter this strange metaphor of the analyst as an obstetrician, the afterbirth of a symptom, and the patient who must be a woman, and I suppose a pregnant one at that. The imagined viability of psychoanalysis, its projected completion, is an arousal of a desire that impels the use of a metaphor, that is, to say the least, pregnant with meaning. I'd like to mark that for now and keep going.

With respect to his second category, the progress of authority, Freud says that nothing is more pressing than the craving for authority since the waning of the power of the religions – what he calls the father complex. While he doesn't seem to include himself or psychoanalysis in its lineaments, what is important for Freud at this point in the article is that patients crave it. Freud feels that an increase in the authority of the psychoanalyst must be forthcoming or work with these patients is bound to fail.[12] (Not one or two looked at his modest office and thought to themselves, 'And *you* promise me such a cure?') Society, Freud complains, is not in a hurry to grant this authority, since psychoanalysis destroys its illusions and exposes its injurious effects. With this reversal of the object of attack – first Freud by patients, now society by Freud – he says that he hopes that 'intellect' will overcome self-interest and emotion when they have exhausted their fury. He continues:

> to estimate the increase in our therapeutic prospects when we have received general recognition, you should think of the position of a gynaecologist in Turkey and in the West. In Turkey, all he may do is feel the pulse of an arm stretched out to him through a hole in the wall: and his medical achievements are in proportion to the inaccessibility of their object. But now that the force of social suggestion drives sick women to the gynaecologist, he has become their helper and saviour.[13]

Another metaphor; I'll come back to the gynaecologist as well.

Freud's third reinforcement comes from what he calls the general effect of our work. Freud states that, when the riddle that the instinct presents is solved, these diseases cease to be able to exist – like revealing the name of an evil spirit that has long been kept secret. Naming destroys a spirit's power. So, if we put society in the place of the individual, what has to be attacked is the secondary gain from illness that is granted externally. If this seems utopian, he reminds us that it has already taken place – there are now, thanks to the birth of psychiatry, less visions of the Virgin Mary: since these women no longer create believers or have chapels built in their honour, they bring round the doctors.[14]

For a smaller example, Freud says, imagine a number of ladies have arranged among themselves that when they have to relieve a natural need during a picnic they will state that they are going to pick flowers. If someone exposes this pretence, no lady will think of availing herself of this flowery pretext and will instead admit her natural needs, to which no one will object. He concludes:

> The energies which are to-day consumed in the production of neurotic symptoms . . . will . . . help to strengthen the clamour for the changes in our civilization through which alone we can look for the well-being of future generations . . . you are contributing your share to the enlightenment of the community from which we expect to achieve the most radical prophylaxis against neurotic disorders along the indirect path of social authority.[15]

I do love this essay. It's absolutely wild. What on earth is going on? With each reinforcement of the future prospects of psychoanalysis, we end up encountering a host of sexual associations whose central metaphor is pregnancy and paternity – seed planting, obstetrics, placentas, gynaecological exams, visions of the Virgin, women's secrets, naming of evil spirits, flower picking and prophylaxis. The aim, in the end, is the increasing availability of the feminine object.

What seems important is not so much these associations as a problematic intrusion, but what they signal in terms of what will be worked through by Freud as he moves forward from this juncture. This essay is a jumping-off point for Freud. Whatever this is, embedded in the question of him as the father of psychoanalysis, will be a source of work that will transform both his ideas of psychoanalytic technique and his conception of the future of the field.

4. The birth of psychoanalysis

Many have noted that, early on, Freud seems to equate the unconscious with a woman, and a very resistant one at that.[16] If Freud takes the unconscious as a woman, then it makes sense that the future prospects of psychoanalysis depend on a kind of obstetric and gynaecological mastery, the central struggle for Freud being one between a knowing doctor, as authority, and a resistant woman patient, as object of investigation.

Historical and clinical scholarship on *Studies on Hysteria* (1893–95) and the Dora case (1905), as well as many feminist critiques of psychoanalysis, have covered this ground extensively.[17] I'd like to show that there is in this early Freud something more than merely a struggle between the sexes. There is something too of a critical encounter with desire and its limits.

In Erik Erikson's seminal 1954 paper, 'The Dream Specimen of Psychoanalysis', he analyses Freud's dream of Irma's Injection, understood as the inaugural dream of psychoanalysis analysed in full by Freud.[18] The dream stands at the beginning of the birth of psychoanalysis because it allows Freud to conclude in the *Interpretation of Dreams* (1900) that the dream is a wish. The uncanny similarity of the dream with many of the metaphors in the 1910 paper can be of some use.

To recount, Freud's dream involves Irma, a female patient who was resistant to treatment. Freud, in the dream, is frustrated and guilty (he had been admonished by a colleague the day before the dream for not having cured Irma completely). In the dream, Freud receives Irma at a party, and she complains of pains. He takes her over to the window to examine her and looks into her mouth, where he sees a strange abscess or wound. Suddenly, a series of colleagues appear who opine on the cause of Irma's illness, both accusing and exonerating Freud. Towards the end of the scene, Freud hears and then sees the written formula for her cure, 'trimethylamin', a nonsense word, but whose embedded meanings are important for Freud because he is beginning to conceptualise what is unique about psychoanalysis and separates him from the sway of authority of his medical peers.[19]

Erikson beautifully analyses the dream, looking closely at its linguistic construction and Freud's situation, on the cusp of discovery, at the time it was dreamt. The dream, Erikson points out, begins as a birthday reception in a great hall where Freud receives guests, already foreshadowing this idea of a birth. Erikson links the German *empfangen* to its two roots – 'conception' and 'reception'. There is thus a link in the dream between the intellectual, medical and sexual in the notion of conceptualising, reception and germination of ideas, and a wish for fruition. It is, in a word, 'an imaginary scene of conception'. Furthermore, the dream for Erikson moves from frustration, vagueness as to what plagues Irma, nonsense formulas and diagnoses, to what he calls an 'immediacy of conviction' in harmony with the authorities that are brought in. A fraternal and paternal pact is formed that 'clarifies the past and unburdens the present'. This, Erikson says, should be seen in the opposition between the masculine precision of a bold formula, the one Freud sees clearly before him, and the murky, unyielding, veiled and resistant woman.[20]

Pushing this, Erikson states, the dream then, is just another haughty woman, wrapped in too many mystifying covers and putting on airs. Freud's letter to his friend and mentor Wilhelm Fliess spoke of an 'unveiling' of the mystery of the dream when he subjected the Irma dream to 'exhaustive analysis'. In the last analysis, then, the dream itself, may be a mother image; she is the one, as the Bible would say, to be known.[21]

Freud wrote of the Irma dream in a 1908 letter to his collaborator Karl Abraham: 'Sexual megalomania is hidden behind it, the three women [whom Freud associates with the figure of Irma], Mathilda, Sophie, and Anna, are the three godmothers of my daughters, and I have them all!'[22] We now know that the dream anticipates the birth of Anna, who will grow up to be her father's protector. Freud, in the dream, wants all the women. Even further, the desire is for the object to completely give way, stop putting on 'airs', and give him recourse for the sake of future generations, for the sake of progress, for the sake of the authority of the analyst!

The authors of *Freud's Women* also point out that the Irma dream is logically tied to Freud's *non vixit* dream, whose principle figure is Joseph Paneth, the fiancée of Sophie Paneth – whom Freud, thinking of the dream, felt would be a much better psychoanalytic prospect than the recalcitrant Irma.[23] In the *non vixit* dream, death and immortality, ambition and murderous rivalry, are the pressing themes. Again, children – in particular daughters – and professional success are the keys to immortality.

Freud notes that a particularly infantile wish makes its appearance in the dream – the logic being one he remembers from his childhood of *quid pro quo*, 'an eye for an eye'.[24] Within this logical system the dimension of speech seems paralysed because of the recourse to aggressive action. This is, somewhat uncannily, the logic of Lacan's mirror stage: captured by the image of the other as a rival ego that collapses into an imaginary battle without mediation.[25] The structure of narcissism is transitivistic – the easily exchangeable place of dyadic identification, you–me, subject–object – which makes a third presence (desire) difficult. In the *non vixit* dream Freud vanquishes his rival, Joseph, and is ecstatic to have found himself in 'possession of the field'.[26]

Lacan, in his seminar 'The Other Side of Psychoanalysis' (1968–69), boldly states: there is no such thing as 'all the women'. For Lacan this is the meaning of castration, of the limits imposed upon our narcissism, the impossibility of total satisfaction and possession – either of self or of others. Lacan reads Freud's much misunderstood work, *Totem and Taboo* (1917), as an allegory of this dilemma. At the dawn of civilisation the father is murdered by his sons, transforming the object, i.e. the women, into one that must enter an economy of exchange. The father loses his exclusive reign over the object, but contra Oedipus, so do the sons as well. The primal father is a myth of prehistory that we retain in the form of our omnipotent fantasies.[27]

So while Erikson concludes with his analysis of the father of psychoanalysis, ironically to substantiate his own theory, I'd like to push his line of thought a bit further. The crucial question seems to me to be one concerning the relationship between desire and its object. If the idea is that desire meets with an object that offers satisfaction, can we escape this struggle for authority, the struggle around knowledge, the imaginary battle with a rival, taken in a different way, as a struggle between the sexes? Or does Freud, in imagining that he is giving birth, that he is at the beginning of a long trajectory or progressive movement, driven by a fantasy of immortality, sow the seeds of a confrontation with an inevitable gap, a limit, an impossibility inherent to desire?

In the struggle, there is a victor (Freud) and a loser (Irma, his colleagues, Joseph Paneth, and the like). But Freud cannot remain solely on the side of the victor. In fact, the bodily kernel of the dream that evokes the most anxiety happens in his identification with the victim – when he palpates Irma and eventually looks into her mouth and sees, as Lacan calls it, this horrific sight, an inside-out head, similar to when Freud watches Joseph Paneth completely dissolve in the *non vixit* dream, as an effect of his gaze. What I mean to point out by this is that desire shouldn't be taken merely as a selfish desire to win, to kill, to possess, to conquer, but what in fact transcends these, in so far as desire articulates its own limits; or, as Lacan would put it, desire carries within it the confrontation with the lack, and the piece of the Real, from which it springs.

For Lacan, psychoanalysis is about the ethical and transformative implications of cultivating this work with desire. If Freud was radically inhibited in reality, bereft of his desire, it is the work with these dreams, his self-analysis, which enables him to push forward and to take up his desire beyond the sticky and inhibiting grasp of his narcissistic wishes. This, for Lacan, has more to do with the side of desire that brings the message of 'castration' or 'impossibility' and uniquely, singularly, symbolises that constraint for a subject.

5. Reading Freud's desire

Serge Leclaire, in his book *Psychoanalyzing: On the Order of the Unconscious and the Practice of the Letter*, first published in French in 1968, follows this trail of Freud's desire. In this work, he reads Freud's desire with careful attention to the imagery, language and the formal mechanisms inherent in Freud's dreams. He uses Freud's essay on screen memories, which we know to be autobiographical, along with the biographical material of Freud's life that follows his self-analysis – particularly that which comes to the fore in the letters with Fliess.

Leclaire, going back over the early Freud, charts out the subtleties of his desire using its linguistic and what he calls its phantasmatic or Oedipal components. He notes the closeness of the German word *Laib* ('loaf') in Freud's screen memories to the word *Leib* ('body'), in German acoustically indistinguishable; the image of the people with bird beaks that carry Freud's mother, an image from the Bible his father gave him, his mother's face the image of both death and beatitude, whose cause, Leclaire says, Freud no doubt imagines himself to be. It is, he says, the mother who smiles, or fails to smile, on her hero son. He follows the centrality of the book torn to shreds at the bidding of Freud's father in the dream of the Botanical Monograph, much like the flowers Freud ripped from the hands of his first love, Pauline, in the screen memory, and the devouring of his favourite flower, the artichoke.[28]

Leclaire finds circulating again and again the formula of Freud's desire – to rip, tear, reveal, pick, pluck. We can see the intricate relation: book and woman; dream and woman;

leaf – flower – pages – petals – defoliation – picking – eating – plucking – tearing.[29] If Freud wanted to tear or rip the veil off the secret of dreams, the phantasmatic portion of that desire – by which I mean the impossible image of its Oedipal satisfaction, the one that holds out the promise of fulfilment and mastery notably in an act of devouring, ripping into the object – suggests that we cannot follow Freud there.

What Leclaire wants to underscore is that Freud reveals to us the secret of dreams as unconscious desire, which is not equivalent to a haste towards the object. The object is not available to desire like a book to be torn apart (what Leclaire calls the substitute that Freud's father offered to Freud for his Oedipal phantasm).[30] Freud got into difficulty with books in his adolescence, amassing debt by purchasing them on credit, a first neurotic symptom. Leclaire will say that what psychoanalysis teaches us is that desire in its purest formal sense is a desire for transgression, for a movement that goes beyond, beyond even its object – but which it cannot surpass. So one must pass through the castration complex, reconcile oneself with a desire that cannot completely accommodate itself to this object that seems to hold it captive. There is desire, and there is the object that causes desire.[31]

If psychoanalysis is making manifest the truth of desire, it is the tragic truth of the asymmetrical relation between desire and the object. For Leclaire, psychoanalysis must shift its fascination with the object of desire to desire itself, in order to proceed psychoanalytically. It must give up the phantasmatic object that it believes will satisfy, gratify or suture desire, as some imaginary end point – the illusion of the object that will make it whole. Following this, there is no truth for us beyond unconscious desire; beyond it is only an unknown, a navel, a floor, which causes desire to be constantly reborn.

It is to this desire that the subject accommodates him or herself, not vice versa. We accommodate the subject to desire, not desire to the subject. Progress, as Freud imagines it in his early essay on the future, means the latter, which forces

the metaphor of an obstetric struggle, the doctor forcing
the woman to open herself to him. The appearance of the
transgressive object seems to offer unsurpassed satisfaction,
mastery and authority, like the infantile love for little Gisela
that brings Freud's desire to its highest pitch. We know it
was this love that made Freud fall into his first depression. It
implies, among other things, the necessity of mourning and
working-through. Perhaps, in this line of thought, psychoanalysis still has a work of mourning to do, not for Freud, as many
claim, but for the consequences of this barrier to the object.

6. Freudian endings

There is something of a kind of working-through that can be
located in Freud – an encounter and work with desire and its
limits. It changes his relationship to the future, in particular,
to the future of psychoanalysis. When tracing how Freud's
model changes from the 1910 paper onward, a radical shift
can be seen. I did a little study of all other uses of the word
'future' in Freud and I think you will not find another paper
like the one on the 'Future Prospects'. The next time Freud
takes up the subject is in his 1919 paper 'Lines of Advance in
Psycho-Analytic Therapy', given in Budapest at the end of
the First World War and after what he calls a 'long and difficult separation'. He says he feels 'drawn to review the position
of our therapeutic procedure'.[32] His tone has changed, to say
the least.

He begins, 'we have never prided ourselves in the com-
pleteness and finality of our knowledge and capacity'.[33] The
ethic he will introduce in this lecture, interestingly, is one
of abstinence. Like an Oedipal prohibition it seems to mark
some fundamental boundary setting up the conditions
of privation and neutrality as essential to psychoanalytic
practice. While he is speaking of technique, one must hear
this in light of the Oedipal object which haunts his work in

'Future Prospects', and which Leclaire frames in his analysis of Freud's desire.

Parenthetically, we can imagine that the response of the field to this ethic of abstinence – from flagrant disobedience, à la Ferenczi and Jung, or, on the flipside, the rigid distant coldness that many interpreted it to decree, both of which have caused such a severe backlash over recent decades – has something to do with this Oedipal phantasm which Freud was in the processes of working through. The next generation of psychoanalysts respond with disregard or mechanical distance – too close, too far.

Freud states very forcefully, 'we refused most emphatically to turn a patient who puts himself into our hands in search of help into our private property, to decide his fate for him, to force our own ideals upon him and with the pride of a Creator to form him in our own image and see that it is good. I still adhere to this refusal.'[34]

Concluding, he says that he will allow himself to 'cast a glance' at a situation which belongs to the future. As many know, he hopes that psychoanalysis will at some point adapt itself to work with the poor. It might mean some changes, but these will always take their most effective means from a 'strict and untendentious' psychoanalysis.[35] I cannot help but hear in this Freud's having taken the desire for creation out of the equation, its violence, the pregnancy fantasy. The desire to look behind the veil is reduced to an ethic of abstinence, which is, contrary to what many claim – most notably relational analysts – predicated on the fall of the authority of the analyst, the fall of his desire for mastery. This substitution is not something in the order of a fullness of knowledge, authority, or the progressive movements of an army of psychoanalysts. You no longer hear about the authority of the analyst, only the authority of the unconscious, of the work in the direction of elaborating unconscious desire in its dimension of singularity.

The implication is the one I've learned from Lacan

– namely, that the unconscious is not simply what is not conscious, and even what might be made conscious, a kind of annexing of alien territory, female or conceptual, but something more radical. The bar is drawn. Mastery, as in sexual mastery or any other, is a fantasy. That fantasy, as in analysis, has the possibility of revealing to us our desire in a singular fashion and is at the heart of psychoanalytic working-through. I feel as if I can palpably hear it: the mention of the long, difficult separation, the negation of pride, the stress on incompleteness, transience, the poor.

The change that takes place between 'Future Prospects' and 'Lines of Advance' is not a linear progress of knowledge. It should be seen as a shift in Freud's subjective position with respect to unconscious desire; a shift that takes place precisely because of a deepened work with the notion of fantasy; bowing, as he says in the 1919 paper, before the superior forces of the unconscious.[36] In its way, it constitutes a reckoning with the castration complex in the Lacanian sense of traversing the phantasm and a work of mourning with respect to the object.

To conclude with Freud, I know that we all know the value of openness, but I hope I have drawn a picture of its place as a specific psychoanalytic truth that has formidable bearing on this anxiety about the future. Progress can become an ideology marked by an implicit failure to work with unconscious desire. As Terry Eagleton says in *Reason, Faith and Revolution*:

> An excess of light, as Edmund Burke knew, can result in darkness; a surplus of reason can become a species of madness. A form of rationality which detaches itself from the life of the body and the affections will fail to shape this subjective domain from the inside . . . The ideology of progress, for which the past is so much puerile stuff to be banished to the primeval forests of prehistory, plunders us of our historical legacies, and thus of some of our most precious resources for the future.[37]

Eagleton goes on to quote Theodor Adorno who, much in the same vein as Freud, states that 'it would be advisable to think of progress in the crudest, most basic terms: that no one should go hungry anymore, that there should be no more torture, no more Auschwitz. Only then will the idea of progress be free from lies.'[38] Lacan understood this in a powerful way.

Dream Life

The relationship between critical theory and French clinical psychoanalysis, in particular between the figures of Theodor Adorno and Jacques Lacan, runs in my mind like one long missing scene in a grand movie – a movie in which the pair seem to discover one another as lost brethren, circling around one another without ever really meeting. The divide has a lot to do with the aftermath of the Second World War, and the exile of the – mostly German – critical theorists in the United States and problems around the relationship to Martin Heidegger because of his ties to National Socialism. Jürgen Habermas turns against psychoanalysis, while the French, lagging behind German philosophy and psychoanalysis after the war, finally are in need of no one – such is their arrogance. Psychoanalysis splinters institutionally, Lacan is forced out of the International Psychoanalytic Association, and psychoanalysis as a clinical practice becomes irrelevant to academia. The last traces of psychoanalysis are more and more professionalised, resembling little the psychoanalysis that concerned either Adorno or Lacan.[1] Adorno dies in 1969, Lacan dies in 1981. One with a ball of string, the other with headphones on.

And yet, how can we not couple Adorno and Max Horkheimer's *Dialectic of Enlightenment* (1944) with Lacan's *Kant avec Sade* (1963)? Two of the most astounding works on the question of civilisation, the contradictions of the Enlightenment, and the theology of progress whose fog still envelops us. The incessant problems that haunt reason, especially the vicissitudes of morality, guilt and the super-ego, are still found as plain as the day in most neurotic cycles of violence. In the darkness of the current moment of psychoanalysis – a practice in decline, marginalised, without the energy of invention, carrying an abominable history of ethical misconduct, and whose institution is fully clerical in both the religious and bureaucratic sense – I long for what was at stake in the question of psychoanalysis for these two figures.

Psychoanalysis in Paris was galvanised around the events of May 1968, having failed to cohere much before this time in comparison to the legions of analysts and new analytic theories in the United States and the UK. While the critical theorists continued to dream in exile about the possibilities and contradictions of thought itself in the contemporary landscape, abandoning the project of psychoanalysis as a wistful idea of a cure from a time before Auschwitz, the French psychoanalysts, exiled from the main institutional body of the post-Freud institution, would begin to heavily emphasise the radical exile of the Freudian subject. One can think of these as two responses to the war, two responses to exile.

For Walter Benjamin and Adorno, thinking had to be a melancholic science, a work of mourning with no final unity or purging of the dead in concert with a history of unspeakable atrocities. Benjamin spoke of writing as a writing of the ruin, rescuing the luminous fragments of life discarded by the seamless narrative of progress and reason. For Adorno, aphorism took on a certain power, mirroring the fragmentation of the world. He developed the non-hierarchical paratactic style, hoping to create a work that was not an object of easy consumption or propaganda, a work in which the position of subject and object vacillated wildly.

The French psychoanalytic version of critical theory reverses course with this project: melancholia as a cure for predatory reason is, for Lacan, the forced choice between violence or melancholia in an unjust world. Instead, Lacan wanted to emphasise a third choice, one he found in the invention of a psychoanalytic cure, the way in which a symptom could become a way of living, an ethos or ethical stance, that signals a final disenchantment, a confrontation with the limits of illusion.

Even if the world induced melancholia, desire had to be strong, precisely in the face of difficult truths. For Lacan, what *is* can never be an excuse for the abandonment of one's desire, which in one sense defines melancholia and neurosis. Lacan is not judging people suffering from depression, he is making a psychoanalytic point: for melancholics and neurotics alike there is a necessity to hear and put to work their desire in the world, broken though it is. The analyst does not cure by authority but rather through its subversion. Abstinence defines the position of the analyst faced with a patient's craving for an abuse of authority, what legislates the authoritarian personality. Power manifests in order to keep desire under repression, and desire undermines the dynamics of power.[2] *How can you not see in the most perverse of fantasies the attempt to open our self to the pain of existing as such, the pain of being a sexual being?*, Lacan asks.

To be a subject – stemming from the Latin *subiectum* – is literally to be 'thrown-under'. Desire is involved with an original loss. The Anglo-American Freud seeks to adapt desires, force compromise formations, cure melancholia, just enough, so that one can be successful. The problem for both Adorno and Lacan was not simply one of thought overcoming itself, nor of the proletariat overcoming their enslavement, but a particular kind of Freudian impossibility in the attempt at any overcoming or self-realisation. The division, the point of loss, simply cannot be overcome. Work with desire overturns a melancholia that was a just, but never final, response to a formidable social hell, to a 'fraternity' to which man never measures up. Reviving the dream of this joint project of psychoanalysis and philosophy – a melancholic science and a science of melancholia – perhaps we can find again the unique vision of a psychoanalytic cure that also offers a palpable diagnosis of the ills and discontents of our current civilisation, the one pointed to by these works written so much in concert on Sade and Enlightenment morality.

Adorno dreams

Adorno kept a dream journal between 1932 and 1969. This he intended for publication, but it was only published posthumously, in 2007, under the title *Dream Notes*.[3] I don't know of another philosopher who has chronicled his dreams in such length and detail. Perhaps the only rival to this dream journal is Freud himself.

We don't know what use Adorno wanted to make of this transcription of his dreams over thirty-seven years, only having his meticulously kept notes (transcribed by his wife). Only two parenthetical notes – quoted by the editors of the book – indicate something of his thoughts about this record of his dream life. Adorno writes, 'Certain dream experiences lead me to believe that the individual experiences his own death as a cosmic catastrophe.' And, 'Our dreams are linked with each other not just because they are "ours", but because they form a continuum, they belong to a unified world, just as, for example all Kafka's stories inhabit "the same world". The more dreams hang together or are repeated, the greater the danger that we shall be unable to distinguish between them and reality.'[4]

What possible critique might Adorno's dream journal offer to psychoanalysis, especially in its eschewal of any associations or interpretations; Adorno's insistence on making present this continuum-in-itself? And finally what might psychoanalysis offer to a reading of a philosopher's dreams?

Adorno's dreams are a kind of testament to the difficulties he suffered after the Second World War. The dreams certainly consist mostly of nightmares. If dreams are the fulfilment of wishes, one might feel hard-pressed to find the wish buried beneath the 'nauseating' anxiety of Adorno's dreams. Many of these dreams took place when Adorno was in exile between 1941 and 1949 in Los Angeles, a city he found both fascinating and horrifying. Adorno's many works on the culture industry as a kind of barbarism that was verging on fascistic hypnosis of the masses – blinding them to the dire situation of the world[5] – is reflected in dreams of celebrity-filled parties whose promise of untold pleasures becomes an inescapable labyrinth in his dream life. In these dreams Adorno never achieves the desired enlightenment of the masses, though he tries, and he finds it difficult to make himself even remotely understood. Indeed, the dream journal may have been an attempt to stay in touch with this inner unity during a period of historical fragmentation and banishment from home. The journal, as a document of an important thinker's dream life, is extremely suggestive and – in its incomparable uniqueness – of immense value.

There is also something important to consider about his two parenthetical statements on dreams. They serve as a neat indicator of how to map Adorno's philosophical work with the very project of psychoanalysis that founds itself on the work and meta-psychology of dreams. The fact of death *is* experienced as a cosmic catastrophe and every nightmare or anxiety dream is an attempt at working through not only trauma, but also the acceptance of one's mortality and the fragility of life. Dreams help us confront what Lacan called the Real, which he defined as the impossible – the impossible to think, the unspeakable and unsymbolised, the object of anxiety *par excellence* wrapped in various imaginary guises from death, to the female genitalia, to castration. Many have spoken of the Real as what erupts in trauma – the sudden uncanny presence of the sheer materiality and mortality of the body. Certainly in Adorno how we accept mortality and the trauma of history is of undue importance.

That dreams are linked to one another and form a continuum in the logic and structure of the unconscious – thereby demonstrating a kind of unity – is as close to a Lacanian theory of the Other as one can find in Adorno. The Other is a kind of unity, one that makes its appearance in dreams, slips of the tongue, free association, transference. It forms a world that is uniquely ours, the sedimentation of history in language, though we have no direct access to it. However, it is not just ours, since the Other is tied to language, history and culture, thus uniting the individual with the fabric of the social order. Of course, Adorno being Adorno, he worries that this unified world will become present prematurely, or just simply become too present. One might think of this as the problem with psychosis. But contrary to this assumption, from the point of view of psychoanalysis, the problem is that for the majority of us neurotics, this world, this Other scene, is not present enough. We are always too deaf and too blind to it. The cure is not in the taming or expulsion of the Other, but in establishing commerce with it. How is this to be done?

It is always on the edge of this kind of paranoia in Adorno that psychoanalysis and his version of critical theory are at odds with one another; his critique too excessive in my opinion, where he fails to see another side to the work of psychoanalysis. Adorno writes in his dream journal that his wife asked him why he makes fun of himself in dreams, and he replied without thinking, 'to fend off feelings of paranoia'.[6] So he recognises the problem (though only after his wife has called it to his attention). It is important to understand this dividing line between a paranoid relation to the Other and a theoretical praxis in relation to it. If we ignore the last statement about the danger of dreams hanging together too much and distorting reality, I think we see Adorno's profound recognition of the importance of the unconscious, how contact with dream life is a confrontation with desire that can inform an ethical form of thinking and creativity (à la Kafka). This work serves as a foundation for both critical thought and a curative ethos. I will demonstrate this through a reading of some of his key dreams.

Dreams are ingenious, and of course on several occasions Adorno's dreams are absolutely brilliant in a manner befitting his way of thinking and seeing the world. On 10 September 1954 Adorno writes: 'I dreamt I had taken part in a theological discussion . . . A speaker expounded the distinction between "equibrium" and "equilibrium". The former was inner balance, the latter, outer balance. The effort of proving to him that there was no such thing as equibrium was so great that I woke up in the attempt.'[7]

The lack of 'equibrium' is not only the central content of the dream but is contained in its formal structure as well, since the effort to prove the falsity of the speaker's statements is so great that it wakes Adorno up, meaning he loses his inner balance. The way in which form follows content is what makes the dream funny. But behind this humour one can also hear a wish, the wish for something impossible that appears at the point of nonsense, the signifier 'equibrium'. The signifier points to an absence or lack, evoking desire.

For Adorno, this absent thing is profaned by the speaker's theological extrapolation on what he assumes simply *is*. But it *isn't*. That is what Adorno is at such pains to get across. Much of Adorno's thought is directed at this impossibility: 'If wrong life really cannot be lived rightly . . . then for that very reason there can be no correct consciousness . . . in it either.'[8] The impossibility has to be contained in thought, even if it means paradoxical thought, for example the truth of the dream being that there is no 'equibrium', which nonetheless does not exist.

The same logic is at work in one of my favourite dreams, dreamt much earlier than the latter, sometime in November 1942 in Los Angeles. Adorno dreams:

> I was talking with my girl-friend X about the erotic arts with which I thought her conversant. I asked her whether she had ever done it *par le cul* ['up the arse']. She responded very frankly, saying that she could do it

on some days, but not on others. Today was a day when it was quite impossible. This seemed quite plausible to me but I wondered whether she was speaking the truth or whether this was just a prostitute's pretext for refusing me. Then she said that she could do quite different things, more beautiful things, Hungarian ones, of which I had never heard. In reply to my eager questioning, she said, 'Well, there was Babamüll, for example.' She started to explain to me. It soon turned out that this supposed perversion was in reality a highly complicated, to me entirely opaque, but evidently illegal finance operation, something like a safe way of passing worthless cheques. I pointed out to her that this had nothing to do with the erotic techniques she had promised me. However, she stuck to her view and replied in a supercilious tone that I should pay close attention and be patient – the rest would come of its own accord. But since I had completely lost track of the connection, I despaired of ever finding out what Babamüll was.[9]

The series formed around the signifier 'Babamüll' is fascinating and hilarious: *Müll* means 'garbage' or 'waste' in German, *baba* is clear in its reference to babies, bottles, orality. Together, they are a promised erotic art to supplement for the impossibility of anal sex, a sexual act that turns out in the end to be some kind of 'illegal finance operation' like 'passing worthless cheques'.

How can we not think of Freud's unconscious series baby=penis=faeces=money.[10] Adorno wants an anal-erotic, not to mention exotic, encounter. It is not in the least accessible or available – 'quite impossible', as his girlfriend says – and the greater his anticipatory excitement, the less comprehensible his situation feels. The series, as Freud defines them, are drive representatives that appear in the place of what is irrevocably lost. Following these avatars of drive and desire, one slides down the chain of signifiers as they already exist

formed in the unconscious network of wishes. This momentum in Adorno's dreams often leads to the concrete need for
some transgressive-excessive act (*par le cul*). Adorno grows
over-excited or desperate. The lost object appears as waste,
garbage, an abortion, something psychoanalysis has always
linked with melancholia: the identification with what falls,
what is rejected, what is trapped in an impossible exile, what
we must achieve radical separation from. It is for this reason
that Freud, when contemplating melancholia, wondered if
one needed to be this sick in order to see this truth.[11]

Adorno must be patient, so he seems to say to himself.
The object will only come in its own time, of its own accord.
He is scolded superciliously by his girlfriend – 'Be patient!
Pay attention!' But what we find is Adorno's haste towards this
object, or obstinate distance, and his refusal to play a game of
interchanging desire – the desired anal sex for your Babamüll
– causes a kind of breakdown. One is trying to get one over on
the other. Nevertheless, it would be a mistake to believe that
his paramour's lesson is lost on him, for Adorno often spoke
about the necessity of letting the unique time-stamp of the
object speak, one of his reasons for loving music as much as
he did.

Adorno's diagnosis of the contemporary world as an
impossible bureaucratic regulation of life in the model of a
Kafkaesque labyrinth is powerfully represented by this dream:
the erotic degrades into anal exchange, gold turning into shit,
which becomes an endless paper stream, the fraudulence of
currency. The world feels unnavigable. Perhaps the difference between this early dream and the 'equibrium' dream is
that the signifying point of nonsense is less a point of despair
than it is in this one, saturated with the unfulfilled promise
of erotic satisfaction. It must be said that the 'prostitute' and
her Babamüll appears in one of Adorno's last dreams. This
time she is 'Mistress A', who demands he buy a 'prick washing machine' if he wants her to have sex with him with her
mouth. He thinks to himself that she might be a saleswoman

for the firm that manufactures the machine, and wakes up laughing.[12] Perhaps here, Adorno's projected anality finds its point of humour.

It is important to note that while these dreams may be funny to us, especially in their lewdness, it's unclear – or, rather, uncertain – as to how funny they are to the Adorno in the dream. The anxiety of being deprived, of being duped and led on, seems to me to characterise Adorno's philosophical thought at its worst, namely when paranoia is the only means for him to maintain his integrity. It is always where the signifier appears, implicating Adorno's desire, that one sees another possibility; a challenge to the disorder of the world. And this isn't simply laughing at the corruption made present in the figure of the woman, but rather a kind of refiguring of reality . . . what is this promised but elusive object? Babamüll, prick washing machine, equibrium.

This was in large part *the* fascination I felt while reading Adorno's dream journal: watching possibility experienced by the Adorno in the dream as a space of failure, while the dream itself, the subject that isn't quite Adorno, points the way beyond. I wanted to know more where the dream seems to announce something new and opaque. What comes forward is not Adorno as Adorno in the dream, or Adorno the philosopher, but the unconscious as subject, the one determining or writing this text, that overturns everything.

Certainly, Adorno's writing, and his analyses of literature, are works that seek to give room to this Other subject, non-identity, the object. Adorno felt there was 'a further language "beneath the helpless language of human beings"', but this may be 'no more than the invocation of what doesn't work and can't work'.[13] He sees that there is a language beneath, a second language that concerns an almost inevitable structural failure. But the slant is often more on the melancholia of this failure, than its potential – especially in his dreams.

Dream cure

I'd like to turn to one of the last dreams in Adorno's dream journal as a dream of the psychoanalytic cure, as a way to push the problem of reconciliation. There is a kind of coming to terms with this Other – the unconscious – and our permanent exile from it that need not demand our hypervigilance or paranoia. The dream also unleashes a powerful symptomatic response in Adorno that – if I haven't completely overstepped my bounds as a psychoanalyst (one needs to be careful in reading a text that will never be the same as the speaking presence of a patient) – might become a critical marker for the problems of this joint project of philosophy and clinical psychoanalysis.

The dream in question occurs in Frankfurt at the end of December 1959. Adorno dreams:

> Execution dream. Beheading. Not clear if my head was to be chopped off or guillotined. But so as to keep it still, I placed it in a groove. The blade scraped away at my neck, unpleasantly trying it out. I asked the executioner to spare me this and get on with it. The blow fell but I did not wake up. My head was now lying in a ditch, as was I. I waited on tenterhooks to see whether I would go on living or whether after a few seconds all thought would be extinguished. Soon, however, there would be no doubt of my continued existence. I observed that my body was gone, but that I was still there, quite apart from my head. I also seemed capable of perception. But I then discovered to my horror that every avenue through which I might show myself or communicate had been completely cut off. I thought to myself that the nonsensical nature of belief in spirits was that it suppresses the decisive factor, the very thing that characterises pure spirit, namely its absolute invisibility, and that it thereby betrays spirit to the world of the senses. Whereupon I awoke.[14]

In allowing, even prompting, his own beheading, Adorno confronts the possible extinguishment of all thought and consciousness. It is also a confrontation with a repeatedly imagined trauma that permeates most of his dreams. This is the best that we can hope for from a patient – especially those who procrastinate an encounter and fuel further alienation, protecting desire by never allowing it to find a new source of renewal. The message of the dream seems to me to be that life is possible without the supremacy of the head! One must let this Other scene speak.

Adorno is on tenterhooks to see if he will go on living. And he does, quite apart from his head. While he can perceive, to his horror he finds out that he cannot show himself or communicate. What emerges is a kind of bi-directional truth. What is lost cannot manifest in what we know as the modes of appearance through the senses – showing, communicating. From the other side, thought through consciousness and the senses aimed at this inaccessible thing, betrays its very spirit of invisibility.

Adorno seems surprised in the dream by his final paradoxical thoughts: 'I thought to myself that the nonsensical nature of belief in spirits was that it suppresses the decisive factor, the very thing that characterises pure spirit, namely its absolute invisibility, and that it thereby betrays spirit to the world of the senses.' This dream contains a passage beyond the reliance on reason and hypervigilance; a confrontation with the contradictions of wanting to be understood or to be seen, or to see and understand. The dream is a dream of the precariousness not only of the body, but also of the spirit as the absolutely concealed nature of the object-in-and-for-itself, the object as *das Ding*. This is the object that Adorno worries about in the contemporary world where nothing is sacred, nothing is allowed to stay invisible for long. The object maintains dignity, paradoxically, through Adorno confronting a lack of his own.

Adorno seems to me to be somewhere different by the end

of the dream, rendering to the object its invisibility, through imagining his death. Adorno writes in *Aesthetic Theory*:

> The dignity of nature is that of the not-yet-existing; by its expression it repels intentional humanization. This dignity has been transformed into the hermetic character of art, into – as Hölderlin taught – art's renunciation of any usefulness whatever, even if it were sublimated by the addition of human meaning. For communication is the adaptation of spirit to utility . . . What in art-works is structured, gapless, resting in itself is an afterimage of the silence that is the single medium through which nature speaks.[15]

To strive for this 'silence' that lets speak – and how can we not identify silence with the image of the analyst? – is the dignity of the object that is bartered away by reason, or meaning, or human use.

On the cusp of this kind of transformation and renunciation, finding himself dead, headless – resting in himself – Adorno can push his melancholic science towards the psychoanalytic cure for melancholia, the medium through which 'nature' can finally speak or find its voice, or remain simply in the dignity of a kind of silence. This silence always bears a relation to death, and, following another execution dream in Adorno's dream journal, the condemned – another man – survives his execution with his skeleton aglow, and Adorno awakes with the sound of the singed corpse singing at the top of its lungs. This sonorous moment seems absolutely joyful.

The beheading of philosophy and psychoanalysis

Lacan's subject of the unconscious, and the Adorno beyond Adorno, is an acephalic (headless) subject whose ego is eclipsed, guillotined. One of Lacan's primary examples of this structure can be found in his reading of Freud's dream of Irma's Injection: the dream described earlier as the inaugural dream of psychoanalysis, the dream specimen. Adorno's dream has uncanny resonance with Lacan's interpretation of the Irma dream, which announces, for Lacan, the birth of the psychoanalyst as the possibility of excavating unconscious desire. Of course the fact that both dreams involve this structural beheading seems crucial.

For Lacan, Freud's inaugural dream has a twofold movement. The first occurs when Freud peers into Irma's mouth and finds the peculiar wound in her throat. Lacan says that Freud confronts the flesh one never sees as a revelation: *You are this which is so far from you, this which is the ultimate formlessness.* At the point of this horror, at which most would have awoken, the dream then turns to pure speech and there is no Freud any longer. There is no one who can say 'I'. All the images of Freud's ego – man, head of the household, doctor, father, authority – are eclipsed, as the clown doctors begin to yell out their comical diagnoses. Thus the dream begins in the reception hall, turns towards Irma's mouth, the horrifying object appears, and then the visible world disappears in a hubbub of false speech or doxa. Only then, Lacan says, can another voice be heard, accouncing the solution to Irma's illness, the injection of 'trimethylamin', the formula for which Freud sees in bold print before him. The voice is not Freud's, but one coming from some beyond.

What is fascinating about trimethlyamin is that through Freud's associations and facts derived from biographical data, we know that it stands literally for psychoanalysis: Freud's transferential relationship to Wilhelm Fliess; drive in the form of sexual substance; a powerful premonitory theory of hormones; the purified signifier (in so far as it means nothing, it shows the essence of meaning); the surface of sexuality; and literally the number three ('tri') that has such a crucial place in psychoanalytic theory from the Oedipal triad, to the tripartite structure of the mind, to Freud's many threefold titles, from *Inhibitions, Symptoms, Anxiety* to *Remembering, Repeating and Working-Through*.

We know that Freud, following the writing of *The Interpretation of Dreams* (1900), was more able to abandon his problematic relationship to Fliess, whose paranoid theories and medical malpractice lay behind Freud's guilt in the Irma dream. After *The Interpretation of Dreams*, Freud's courage was less dependent on the approval of an untarnishable authority that induced paranoia and blind submission or fantasised revenge. Freud's relation to authority became less disembodied and super-egoic.

Trimethylamin functions as what Lacan calls a purified signifier of desire, and because of it Freud 'makes himself heard by us' without having even wanted to, without even having recognised what he was saying: 'I wanted to be, myself, the creator, I am not the creator. The creator is someone greater than I. It is my unconscious, it is this voice which speaks in me, beyond me.'[16] Because of this dream, the cure will never be tied in the same way again to the clown-car band of doctors, a cure by medical authority, nor will it be tied to Freud's aggregate of identifications with the complaints of the palpated female patient, including the demand that the cure be sexual, that patients provide Freud with satisfaction or recognition. The dream unravels the mirror in which Freud sees himself – the good doctor, the head of the household – and his women, namely as resistant objects who ought to comply with showing him how he wants to be seen. Of course I am thinking here about the ways that women appear in Adorno's dreams.

Looking at Adorno and Freud's dreams together, we might speculate about the relation between the two moments in the dream – an encounter with this strange wound and the possibility of this solution. Shades of this structure can be found in many figures of contemporary thought. Damaged life is the last contact with an ancient wound in Adorno, which is the basis of the revolutionary character of the art-work. Georges Bataille's *acéphale*, the headless man, isn't merely the walking wounded, he is also a symbol for a whole host of solutions in the form of the sublime lowerings of excess and sovereignty – shit, flesh, sacrifice, atheology and non-knowledge.

I hope the reader can see the importance of Adorno's guillotine dream, in its extraordinary connection with Freud's dream of Irma's Injection. There is a denouement to Adorno's dream that I have not mentioned. Adorno, after the behead-ing dream, immediately has a second dream, a nightmare in fact, in which he has to urinate, 'desperate and full of anxi-ety that I would be unable to control myself'. He finds a uri-nal festooned with flowers for a ladies' party, into which he urinates, causing a huge flood, urinating 'without any end in sight'. He awakes 'with a feeling of horror'.[17]

It is a moment that psychoanalysts would tend to think of as an intense symptomatic urethral *jouissance*, literally as if the phallus is reasserting itself after his beheading. The eclipsing of Adorno's ego, I imagine, is reversed by this phal-lic reassertion, this need for control, and the evocation of a limitless bodily horror that submerges desire. The penis here is not an organ of desire, which always includes the vicissi-tudes of loss; the penis is an object of use, namely for urinat-ing. This slippage from sexual desire and the vicissitudes of loss to mere utility degrades sexuality to its functionality and its function as degrading. On the other side, perhaps we hear the classical analysts warning us that incontinence betrays the presence of masturbation fantasies, fantasies of omnipo-tence and power, bursting in on the primal scene. Either way, impotent or omnipotent, what is magical about the execution dream seems to me to devolve in a stream of urine; philoso-phy becomes a festooned urinal.

While Adorno writes powerfully about his own feelings of endless degradation in contemporary life, whose demand for happiness he certainly challenged, the very idea of giving voice to silence, speaking the unspeakable, is closer to possibility than all the dead ends of a foreclosed present. It is this hairpin movement between the two, between impossibility and possibility, between a melancholic science and a psychoanalytic science of melancholia, that I feel is the most difficult line for Adorno to sustain. And, when it breaks, his work for me collapses into forms of judgement and the super-egoic moralism of critique that he always wanted to avoid.

Damaged Life

Patients seem to identify with some part of the apparatus of culture, civilisation and the organisation and administration of life. While all of these parts might be present in every patient to a degree, something comes to the foreground as a primary structure and possibly primal identification. This is the picture of the social that I have from the consulting room and what is in it that is damaged or damages in a precise way: the machine, the seduction of power, the conditions of precarious life, the body and its regulation by technology and medicine, the sado-masochism of the law and abject life, and the endless attempt to construct a form for sex and gender under the constraints of misogyny and the absorption of the family into capitalism. In this, is there a new type of human being? One that consumerism and the culture industry has bested? I don't know. The picture, in and of itself is, for me, ruthless enough. Ruthless, in particular because of the fact that the choice of identification, what Lacan at one time called the 'choice of neurosis', is not a choice at all. It is a choice that is made for you, a result of a set of contingencies surrounding your birth that lead in one direction or another. From this, one has to invent a solution in order to be able to live, a solution that then contributes back to a world that will go on making choices for others that you can't make good on. Damage directs us to this unpayable debt that we inherit as an ethical challenge, not just as a question of pedagogy and culture, social change and social activism, but also the continuing life of psychoanalysis itself.

Action in Analysis

Between 1967 and 1968 Lacan, just after a seminar on 'The Logic of Fantasy', gave a not-so-well-known seminar entitled 'The Psychoanalytic Act'.[1] Prior to this Lacan's work is zeroing in on the fundamental categories of psychoanalysis: ego, transference, drive, objects, repetition, identification, anxiety. After the seminar on the 'The Act', Lacan's emphasis shifts to a question surrounding the particularity of psychoanalysis: what kind of a discourse is it, where does it stand in relation to the sciences, the university, capitalism, what is truth for psychoanalysis, what is the relationship between truth and knowledge, and so on. What I mean to point out by this is that this seminar is a kind of turning point, both a culmination of Lacan's work from 1953 to 1967, and a decisive shift to what follows, namely from 1968 to 1980. That a question of the act creates a decisive shift perhaps already tells us something about the question of the psychoanalytic act, which is meant to create, in its action, a discernible 'before' and 'after'.

In the beginning of this seminar Lacan asks a question about how psychoanalysis has thought of action which seems stretched between linking action to motor activity, the reflex arc and the discharge of tension, on the one hand, and the notion that thinking, on this basis, can be seen as trial action, frustration tolerance, suspension of action in the direction of reflection. The reflex action, as a response to an intolerable stimulus, automatic action, hardly seems like an action at all, and instead is more of a reaction, a form of flight. This, Lacan points out, is then the lining for thinking, which may simply be another name for inhibition, both of which, especially when taken together, seem to be rather the opposite of action, as intentional activity, something that is designed to have an effect.

Lacan says that the model of action in Freud is perhaps best found in something like *The Psychopathology of Everyday Life* (1901), where the symptomatic action of the patient, as a failed act, a half-act, betrays a much fuller action, a possible action in relation to an unknown truth, a truth that is in the process of emerging and which a subject might seize. So we have the bungled act which points towards a more powerful act on the part of the patient, in line with the unconscious or unconscious desire. This action, in this distinct psychoanalytic sense, Lacan says, is paradoxically linked to the exclusion of the sexual act in the sphere of knowledge, giving sexuality its irreducible character as psychoanalytic truth, on the basis of which, Lacan says, Freud places the dimension of the act. This is why action is always transgressive. When it truly functions as action, it means we are forced to cross a certain threshold; that the act always manifests in relation to this unconscious sexual terrain. This is what we help our patients lay hold of.

I would like to bring in Hans Loewald, because both he and Lacan place a certain emphasis on a more radical concept of action and are deeply suspicious not of action – which we see when analysts want to talk about borderline patients, acting-out, symptomatic action, wild transference, unanalysed whatever, and so on – but of inaction, the stopping of action, inhibition, defence, repression, over-interpretation, intellectualisation, and stasis more generally. The analyst and patient seem to fear crossing a certain threshold and for Loewald this is nothing but resistance to the unconscious. For Loewald, language and the ego more generally, like the character of insight, are defensive, inherently so, when not placed in relation to the function of psychoanalysis, which is to make these – speaking, thinking – closer to a creative act. And Loewald uses the word 'act' here to denote that it brings something absolutely new into existence.[2]

The unconscious then, especially in its expression through transference, is absolutely not something primitive, immature or irrational – which is what I take Lacan to mean when he says the unconscious is structured like a language, meaning it is akin to the highest achievements of the human race. So if we see the action of psychoanalysis as sweeping away transference or the unconscious, we are prescribing a sterile version of life; whereas transference in the analytic situation provides the hook for the emergence of the unconscious which is otherwise blocked in life and condemned to live a 'shadow life', as Loewald puts it.[3]

You will not find in Lacan words like growth, adaptation, integration, synthesis, organisation, maturation – you just won't. I don't like these words either. Transference for Loewald is the site of an action that takes place in analysis and allows the emergence of the unconscious as something creative, new and curative. And one must go *as far as possible*.

So many of the trainee analysts I follow suffer from shame in the face of the transference of their patients, and I know this extends to their own transference, to teachers or others. But this is a misguided view of transference based on an idea that transference is something you get over once you've been properly analysed and find your 'maturity' – an idea that I think makes analysts paradoxically *more* susceptible to boundary violations than this vision by Lacan and Loewald. I think what they mean to say is that we should have more transference, know how to use transference, the transference at the heart of the unconscious, this forbidden terrain of sexuality, this creative potency. So transference is put at the centre of any meaningful action in analysis, making this discernible before and after. If we emphasise transference as a way of situating a greater sense of reality or the ability to love in a 'mature' way, whatever that is, this would be a recipe for making analysts feel like frauds the world over, and be terrified of the one action that psychoanalysis has at its disposal.

In service of this I will present one of my most difficult and shameful cases.

The patient was a forty-four-year-old choreographer: I will call her Thea.

Her case was haunted from the beginning by a question of belief. Thea articulated desperately, at times angrily, how much she needed to believe that I believed her, needed me to indicate that we shared the same beliefs, and asked that I validate what she was saying as the truth. She pushed hard in the treatment at these junctures. She told me that she was a compulsive liar as a child, that she would lie in order to see if adults believed her or not, and if they didn't, what punishments they would mete out. But she got lost in her own lies, and still does. She needed something from me with respect to this question about truth.

Thea came to me two years ago after having an abortion with her partner, who was also dating several other women. Very quickly, she made friends with another patient of mine whom she met in the waiting room, someone much younger than her. She imagined that the three of us were going to be in a kind of sisterhood. Eventually the siblingish jealousies and aggressions erupted. She and the other patient stopped talking to one another at the same moment that her partner chose to have a monogamous relationship with one of his other women, at same moment that I refused to go to a performance of hers. And she was furious.

Thea entered into a state of unravel and distress that was alarming. While she had always been a handful, the treatment was now flooded with impossible affect, paranoia, accusations, and finally a series of 'acting-outs' that troubled me greatly. It is this transition through which the act can be understood – within all of this chaos, both hers and mine – that made me think of this case in the context of this question of action in psychoanalysis. Especially since so often I wanted to rely on some of the worst misogynistic clichés in psychoanalysis to dismiss her and what was unfolding: thinking to myself that she was just one of those traumatised borderline hysterics, or a bitter angry it's-too-late hysteric (maybe if she had had a child things would be different?), or, even, a drama queen artist . . . I was thinking all this as a way of dismissing her, which was simply resistance to the truth that was emerging and pulling on both of us.

Thea filled my phone with messages: voice, audio, text, Facebook Messenger. This tie to me seemed to hold her together, although barely. The man and friend leaving her unleashed a kind of rage about the abortion, and she drove herself further and further into affective torment about having lost this child. Here is the series of events that illustrates the psychoanalytic act: Thea's mother came into town for the first time since she had been in treatment with me, and Thea started using poppers to the point of collapsing. This death drive in her felt new to me; different from the suicidal dramatic chaos that generally surrounded her in a static way. She said that she needed poppers in order to breathe, that something was happening in her neck and chest and that they were the only thing that helped. She wanted a kind of break in her head, a way to go unconscious.

I told her that I was not going to act as if she was merely helping herself breathe when she was poisoning herself. We spoke for the first time in depth about her mother's self-destructiveness, her anorexia, the fact that she spoke with her mother day in and day out, but could not be near her. Something happened to her, some excess in her mother was hard to bear.

She then tried to speak to her former partner about her feelings regarding the abortion. He avoided her, she failed to really confront him, and she asked herself in session about not being able to confront him really. In session, she began to protect him and to speak about how they were meant to be, she knew it, and he simply needed time. I asked her, why was he so protected? Why was her rage at the other woman? I pointed out to her that I wondered about her father, whom she never spoke about. She said, 'There were always other women . . . Have I not told you about them?'

The question of her mother being left for these other women, and her mother's violence vs her father's absence, became central in the treatment. Her mother contacted me out of the blue by email to tell me the following story, hoping it would help her daughter: when Thea was three, the mother, her husband, and Thea were at the mother's parents' house to play with a pet guinea pig. The mother was in the basement and heard a noise and came upstairs to find the guinea pig's leg broken. She accused Thea of breaking it, who didn't say otherwise, and from that moment on stopped touching her, or touched her roughly, deciding she was 'the devil's spawn' (her words). About six months later she strangled Thea, had the feeling of wanting to kill her, but let go at the last minute and hospitalised herself. It was in fact the father who had broken the animal's leg, having kicked it. Thea had protected her father. Suddenly the poppers made more sense to me, this paradoxical question of constriction and breath.

I didn't say much about the email; it wasn't clear to me what was true. I also didn't understand my scepticism about its truth. Something was true. It's just not always clear what is true, especially in *this* case. What feels psychoanalytically true is the sequence of events that followed the email. Thea told me that the two times she'd done poppers before were when she had babysitting jobs, and that whenever she got near children she said she felt the overwhelming urge to hit them, and did – something she was deeply ashamed about. It happened when she was a young girl of twelve, and the two other times when she did poppers as a young adult. Especially when men left her, she felt helpless taking care of these children.

I told her I now understood why she got an abortion. She said she was terrified of having her own child and what she would do to it; and this fear we could understand in relation to a history of sexual confusion and violence in a family which could not separate sex from death. For the first time the abortion wasn't just something passive, the problem of a violent or neglectful man who deprived her of a child, a situation she was conned into. The treatment suddenly had a certain arc. There is a line in the sand, before this knowledge, and after its emergence. We have here unconscious truth, sexuality, act.

Interestingly, in the aftermath, a rage at her father emerged. In session, I was contorting my face while she declared vengeance on her father for neglect and always choosing his mistresses, one of whom was especially cruel to her. This woman often prevented her father from calling her. I was listening, but felt a strange annoyance that the previous chain of events was leading to more victimisation and more vengeance. There was also something in the way she spoke, a kind of drama that left me sceptical, or fighting with my scepticism.

She said, 'You don't think I'm right to be angry at him? Why are you making this face, you need to help me and explain your face to me!' I didn't know what to say. I *was* making a face. I was beset with my scepticism with her. I suddenly found myself saying that I understood her anger at him, but that I was getting confused listening to her because it wasn't clear to me what was a response to his failings, what was a response to the normal exclusion of a daughter from an adult parental relationship, and what was a response to some seduction on his part, calling her when the girlfriend was gone, so that instead of losing, which she was consciously saying she felt, she was actually winning. This was my face.

She stopped, thought, and said, 'Oh . . . Why didn't you just say so?' And then a whole story opened up where the place of these girlfriends (very much like Freud's case of Dora and her infatuation with her father's mistress as a way to shore up her sense of herself as a woman) came to the centre. These women often seduced Thea and dropped her, including the last one, who became her father's second wife. In fact, she said that she and this woman were more like the ones having a secret relationship, not the mistress and her father, because she used to drive up and see Thea perform and send her cards, calling her by her stage names, and signing, 'Your fan' – all without telling the father.

Thea certainly did not tell her mother, as she would have been crushed by this. This woman eventually turned on her, told the father that she was 'bad news' and had the father legally adopt her own daughter – a repetition of the incident with the mother where Thea was judged as bad, keeping the parental couple intact. This devastated Thea. Her father's women were beautiful and cool, not like her mother, and she thought they were going to save her. It was at this point that as a young adult she babysat children and started to hit them.

I understood better who I was in the transference – the happy family with two daughters, who suddenly preferred the other younger daughter, the beautiful mother whom she needed to go to her performances but didn't, which felt like a prelude to dropping her. All of this was suddenly more clear in retrospect. What we see then is not only a series of acts which bring a truth to the surface surrounding questions of sexuality, sexual position and identity, as well as the impossible sexual drive as it courses through our body, but an astonishing staging in the treatment, a will to dramatise and repeat in the transference, which together, eventually forces us to believe, to see some part of a truth. Thea, in a sense, is the ultimate receptacle; total receptivity, an intense affective conduit in a kind of hysterical openness that can always seem suspect, dramatic, but that the analyst needs to accept if the truth is to emerge. Psychoanalysis has to harness, against all resistance on the part of the analyst, this aptitude for transference.

Thea holds me responsible and I her. I say this without moralistic overtones about an autonomous ego, or a respectable responsible self, or an idea of mature sexuality, or even any idea of authenticity, but rather for what is at play between us: what Lacan called symptom-partners, which is also a truth about lovers. Thea helps me escape my own project – the therapeutic project – by making it impossible. By desiring the treatment to be psychoanalytic, through me, the symptom is untangled in the direction of what in it – what truth, what action – is hers to have.

She reminds me what it means to be an analyst, and how we locate this vital/lethal place in her body, the ingestion of the pharmakon which is both poison and cure – embodied in the drug that she takes. The pharmakon, in the case of hysteria, is the key to an excess of both life and death in an encounter with these other women, in an encounter with the disorganising presence of sexuality as it is handed down to us. Remember these women did not just unleash their death drive on her, they were also the source and support of her love of performance, choreographic staging of bodies. The other pharmakon in psychoanalysis is the transference, both the key to the cure and also, paradoxically, its biggest obstacle. The analyst has to accept the flurry of action, of transference, believing in what it makes possible. I hear Thea is a very good choreographer.

End Your Analysis!

I'd like to tell you about Freud's five famous case studies because, to my mind, they tell you about the question, if not the necessity, of getting the hell out of analysis.

Little Hans[1]

A phobic four-year-old boy who goes from being a little Don Juan to living in a mythic and animistic world where animals bite and howl and sometimes fall down or sit on you. His father, in an exchange of letters with Freud, conducted Hans's analysis. His mother was Freud's patient and his father Freud's student and their exuberance for 'the professor Freud' was picked up by Hans, who when in trouble for doing something naughty would say, 'It's all well and good since we can write about it to the professor.' Little Hans, brilliant, cannot seem to get his parents to tell him the truth about where babies come from. So he shrouds himself in myths about horses that speak about the pregnant body, insemination and delivery. *Freud* gets stuck on the horse phobia as Hans's fear of his father's punishment for wanting to nuzzle erotically with his mother. What seems most decisive, clearly not this interpretation, is the one moment Hans goes to meet Freud, who situates him in a lineage of men: 'I knew long before you were even born that your father wanted a little boy like you, as his own father wanted him.' 'Does the professor talk to God?' Hans asked his father on the way home. Analysts have speculated that this interpretation was cast like a protective spell, one that saved Hans from his mother, who wasn't, in fact, a figure of erotic yearning, but an intrusive, jealously insecure woman who felt left out of the fraternal pact being established. She left at the conclusion of Hans's treatment and took her daughter with her, who eventually committed suicide. Hans grew up to be one of the key directors at the Metropolitan Opera in New York, still staging stories. It is said that Freud bought Little Hans a rocking horse.

Dora[2]

The only woman whom Freud writes about extensively, Dora is brought by her father to treatment in order that Freud will disabuse her of her wish to separate him from his mistress, whom he denies as such. Dora tells another story to Freud: she is being bartered by her father to his mistress's husband. Freud, to his credit, does not buy the father's lies, but asks Dora a question in the manner of, *Everything you say is true, but what do you want in it?* Freud will not tolerate the complaint of the beautiful soul who bemoans a disorder they fail to see in themselves. He turns Dora inwards. Through her dreams he discovers that she had in fact protected the very mistress she was trying to dispose of, facilitating the affair, making herself its linchpin. *Who does she serve? Who does she protect?* This revelation opens the door to the question of her feminine sexuality – Dora stunned for two hours in front of the Sistine Madonna, whose virginal face is also the image of horror before the Crucifixion. At this she suddenly shuts the door on Freud. 'Did you know this is our last session?' 'How could I know when you haven't told me?' answers Freud. 'I decided a fortnight ago,' she retorts. 'That sounds like a maid's dismissal,' he replies. Jane Gallop famously said that Dora fucked Freud at the door, something she had witnessed with so many women, especially maids, in the patriarchy of the Hapsburg Empire.[3] She left him on the threshold, but having done so, she taught Freud a lesson on the power of transference. How could anyone who 'conjures up the most evil of those half-tamed demons that inhabit the human breast', writes Freud, ten years later, 'expect to come through the struggle unscathed'?[4]

The Rat Man[5]

An obsessional man falls gravely ill because an event, like a perfect storm, condenses the essence of his familial trauma with an already over-excited anal eroticism that he developed as a young man, centred around, of all things, the word 'rats'. Only psychoanalysis can tell a story like this: during army exercises a private – the Rat Man – loses his glasses and is told by his rather cruel captain two things: that he owes money to Lieutenant A for his new pair of glasses, and that there is a particular way of conducting torture in the east, namely by placing a pot of rats on a captive soldier's buttocks, which then bore their way into his anus. Freud unravels the word 'rats' in a year-long analysis, meandering through its personal references to money, death, sex, aggression and religion. The Rat Man's father, he finds out, also owed money to a lieutenant – for gambling debts – when *he* was in the army, which was only paid off by the money he gained in marrying the Rat Man's mother, who was well off, but not, however, the woman he really loved. The Rat Man's mother and father were fixated on this transaction, the basis of every insult and counter-insult slung across the familial field. The rats were the currency of love, embodied in the Rat Man's symptom of believing that if he did thing x, y or z the Rat Man's father and the Rat Man's lover would both be punished with the rat torture. His father, Freud likes to point out with a chuckle, was already dead at this point. What is so beautiful is this symptom ties his father to the image of the lover, and establishes the true parental couple who desire one another for something more than just rat-money. Freud asks the Rat Man not to pay him with rats, but instead to turn these rats into what they were really composed of, namely, *his* desire. The Rat Man went on to marry the woman he loved instead of the woman his mother wanted him to marry for money.

Daniel Paul Schreber[6]

The analysis of the psychotic judge Schreber is the one case study of Freud's not based on one of his actual patients. It is instead an analysis of a memoir written by Schreber after his descent into psychosis, which occurred after he was promoted to the position of presiding judge at the Dresden Higher Regional Court. In his paranoia, God spoke to him through the rays of the sun, monitoring Schreber's bowel movements and other bodily pleasures, intensifying them to the point of pain, while chattering like birds in High and Low German. What Freud learns is that paranoid delusions are curative of a more general destruction by psychosis, where desire retracts inwards, destroying all contact with the world outside. A hook or tie back to the world needs to be created and delusory paranoiac fantasies act like this suture. *This is a lesson for everyone*, one that Freud radicalises – desire creates our place in the world. For Schreber, God was penetrating his body with the sun's rays in order to make him a woman, his bride. Schreber would be impregnated so that he could repopulate the earth. The delusion returned him to the world with an anticipated future. Schreber, stabilised by this belief, soundly makes an argument for his release at a court hearing, aligning himself with the logic of Christ. 'I can be released because I won't act on my delusions. My kingdom,' he says, 'is of another world.' It was logically irrefutable. Schreber went free and lived a quiet life until his death in 1911.

The Wolf Man[7]

Finally, there is for me the most tragic case of Freud's. The Wolf Man, having too much money and too much secondary gain from his illness, cannot really pay, meaning he cannot make the sacrifice of his symptom in the name of his psychoanalysis. Money means nothing to him. He has too much fun living out a dependency on Freud, leading Freud to do something he'll never do again. He forces termination. In three months, no matter what. Like a confession at gunpoint the Wolf Man reveals the keys to his neurosis, not least of which is a haunting primal scene, his parents doing it *a tergo*, his father's penis magically appearing and disappearing into his mother's bent-over body, the Wolf Man watching from a feverish afternoon nap as a child. His desire, sifted through this scene, is embedded in a nightmare of wolves in a tree outside his window peering at him with their castrating gaze. Freud's transposition: *Their gaze is yours, the window opened like your eyes that afternoon.* But this forced remembering doesn't work. The Wolf Man never really recovers his desire out from under this scene. A few years after his analysis ended, he believes his nose is disintegrating and walks carrying a mirror, transfixed by the image of what might disappear. He was analysed for the next sixty years, and, in a strange act of reversal, having lost all of his money after the two world wars, he became something of a charge for the psychoanalytic institution, paid seemingly for having been Freud's famous patient. The painful denouement: he takes on the name that Freud gave him, publishing and painting not as Sergei Pankejeff but as the Wolf Man, merging with his case history.

These are Freud's five cases and for me their stories are ours. They cover the spectrum. You can find yourself in each one of them in the mode of universalising that was Freud's ethic. Which is your desired end? Rat torture, rapture before the

Madonna, the fate of a maid, animism-cum-brotherhood-of-man, the gaze of a pack of wolves, your nose to a mirror, to be a famous child, the spouse of God? All of Freud's patients had to find a way to desire through their symptom, not outside of it.

Part 2

Distrust Improvements

Variations on a Standard

I

'Variations on the Standard Treatment' is one of Lacan's lesser-read papers from the summer of 1954.[1] It takes off from the question of what constitutes the 'standard' psychoanalytic treatment, in order to know what constitutes a variation, and is intent on showing not only that technique has become increasingly dominated by actions that move away from the analysand's speech, but also how, when speaking of 'standards', analysts seem more concerned with 'standing', meaning their own prestige and power. In the paper Lacan puts down some basic principles of his own regarding listening, interpreting and the position of the analyst, and also some surprisingly straightforward guidelines for what is necessary in the training of analysts.

The phrasing of the title deserves mention, for throughout the paper there is a slippage between 'standard treatment' and 'typical cure'. In French the title is *Variantes de la cure-type* and yet both *traitement standard* and *cure-type* are used to convey the norm for psychoanalytic work. While the English translation tends to stick with the words 'standard' and 'treatment', the paper itself tries to effect a displacement from the many accepted notions of treatment toward the specificity of a psychoanalytic cure. 'Standard' feels more formal and normative than 'typical', which still has the colloquial connotation of 'type', as if it were a choice of one among others. Many have commented that this is Lacan's first use of the word 'cure'. So while 'standard' and 'treatment' are the central signifiers in English, 'cure' slips through as the word of great import for Lacan.

Etymologically, 'cure' goes back to the Latin *cura*, meaning 'care', and Lacan moves away from a medical model which sees illness as a momentary perturbation in a system that should be kept homeostatic, to a conception of care or concern that entails something ongoing and whose final aim is not transitory or a return to the norm (or standard), but a new state altogether. 'Care' has two meanings: worries or troubles and concern or attention – care as burden and care as solicitude. Heidegger points to care as stretched between earth and the divine; the burden that pulls you down, and the concern that lifts you up. Care, in this Heideggerian context, is elevated to a mode of Being which solicits us back to ourselves from escape, anxiety, insignificance and alienation. It opens us back towards a sense of time and the future. The play between care and cure, means and ends, feels critical to understanding what is at stake in Lacan's paper. What do we mean by psychoanalytic care and psychoanalytic cure? This is a question of the ethics of psychoanalysis.

There are other hidden virtues to 'Variations on the Standard Treatment', not least of which is the context of the paper, which forced Lacan into a more systematic review of the literature, which makes its appearance in surprising allegiances and detailed readings (often quite critical) of work by major figures like Anna Freud, Edward Glover, Michael Balint, Sándor Ferenczi, Wilhelm Reich and Theodor Reik, and minor figures like Richard Sterba, Alice Balint, Maxwell Gitelson and Robert P. Knight. Lacan's rhetorical style is not as vitriolic as it is in the 1958 technical paper to which it is often compared;[2] he hadn't yet suffered the betrayal of his colleagues at the Société Française de Psychanalyse (SFP). We must keep in mind that the crisis surrounding Lacan's practice of the short session began roughly in 1951. Furthermore, his move away from the Société Psychanalytique de Paris to the SFP took place during the time that he was working on this paper. However, he was still part of the larger community of analysts at the time (he wasn't excommunicated from the

International Psychoanalytic Association until 1963), part of the Freudian body, and not yet forced to be a Lacanian to the extent that he was excluded from the 'authorised' Freudian association. His position was certainly in jeopardy and he was perceived as a threat, but the lengths to which the institution would go could not have been in any way clear in the summer of 1954. Again, the translation of the title from the French *cure* to the English 'treatment' speaks to something important that mirrors this situation: in French, at the time of writing, Lacan could be seen as attempting to effect a displacement from treatment to cure in the direction of his own reading of Freud, in English – reading from the future, he was put in the position of commenting on the standard treatment from the position of deviant.

The field is still riven by certain impasses on the definition of treatment, impasses that Lacan tried to unearth in this paper nearly seventy years ago. His personal exasperation, the gravity of his tone, and the tragi-comedy of mid-century psychoanalysis he depicts, are, on the one hand, absolutely applicable to today's milieu, but on the other hand, given that we are in a new moment defined by the decline of psychoanalysis with its re-marginalisation in the world of both medicine and the humanities, the article can strike one as prophetic *and* pitiful. The psychoanalysts, even as the public and the major institutions abandon them, continue to wage their narcissistic wars of minor differences, without making much of the theoretical headway that Lacan calls for in this paper. As Lacan writes in section I of 'Variations on the Standard Treatment', 'what is at stake is . . . less a standard, than standing', even as that standing has been lost, in part because of the fevered attempt to maintain a position of power and not the pathway of a psychoanalytic cure.[3]

'Standard' implies 'without variation' and yet, in creating a standard one also delimits a margin of variation. To encircle a centre, one must define the outside periphery. The two – standard and variation – are interdependent on one another.

More often than not value becomes a part of this kind of system of measurement, where the standard is good and the deviations are bad or lesser than.

So what are these variations? And what does it mean to be charged with the task of speaking of variation? Mustn't we first know what is the standard, and perhaps even why it is considered the standard, before we can speak about this outside edge? This is the distortion that is intrinsic to the question, what Lacan calls the stopping point that is also a point of entry into the problem. Lacan is asking us not to stop at whatever is vague or seemingly impossible about the question of standards and variations, but rather to see what the distortion illuminates.

Lacan wants to go back to the most basic terms without assuming we know what they mean, from unconscious to drive to transference; to go back and re-read Freud with fresh eyes, return to Freud, and use theory in order to create a more formal and structural understanding of what is at stake in a psychoanalytic cure. Technique was formally standardised by the institution of psychoanalysis simply as a set of rules – five days a week, lying on the couch, do not accept gifts, pay for missed sessions, interpret only in late mid-phase analysis, etc. And what was done was decided without defining the basic tenets of psychoanalysis. This can be seen today when candidates in analytic training conduct what are called 'control analyses' in order to become graduate analysts. The outcome of a proper control case is often entirely dependent on whether the patient comes to the office five times a week and lies down on the couch, or, in a more bureaucratic iteration, has completed a defined number of hours or weeks of therapy in a given year. If this is not the case (for example if a patient comes less, takes a break, decides they want to sit up) and an argument erupts in the overseeing committee as to why it is still a proper 'control' psychoanalysis, the varying positions are often so irreconcilable that the case is liable not to count towards a candidate's graduation. The same problem exists with respect to the candidate's 'training analysis', which is judged not on the basis of its effects, meaning that the candidate seems to know how to occupy the position of analyst with his or her patients, but rather on whether the analyst is properly accredited by the institution and the candidate has complied with hourly requirements of analysis for graduation. This is exactly the problem that Lacan is addressing in this article: how can it be that only a set of formal procedures defines psychoanalysis ... and yet, he agrees that there should be something like the outlines of what a standard psychoanalytic treatment entails. But not even the psychoanalysts seem to know!

The analyst is taught from the get-go to be wary of any 'haste in concluding' or hastened attempt to cure, meaning that improving is not even on the agenda for the analyst;[4] nor is any certain knowledge concerning diagnosis or aetiology. Psychoanalysts cannot be concerned with improvements or fact-finding, for these could function as a powerful ruse in a treatment. A 'transference cure', which Freud defined as a moment when a patient's symptoms suddenly disappear early in treatment as a way of avoiding the work of analysis, is clearly a false cure. It is a cure in the transference, as a moment of transference (in order not to have to face analysis, to prove the analyst right or wrong, to hide one's symptoms from the analyst's watchful eye, etc.) and so not a real cure, which involves a more fundamental structural change.

Lacan often makes this point, I think because it is so fundamentally counterintuitive and peculiar to psychoanalysis: we are taught not to care if our patient's symptoms improve. In fact, we are taught to distrust improvements more often than not. As well, patients tend to get much worse in treatment before they get better. So the psychoanalyst is someone who makes you sicker, distrusts you if you get well, and, to take this one step further, is taught to be deeply suspicious of any desire to cure in him or herself, what Lacan, following Freud, names *furor sanandi*, the 'rage to cure'.[5] He goes on to say that Freud himself was so deeply worried by a potential desire to cure that, if there was an innovation in technique that seemed based on this desire, he immediately raised the question, 'Is that still psychoanalysis?'[6] So here, the question of standards and deviations points not to a formalism in technique, but rather a formalisation in the analyst, whereby the analyst purifies himself of the desire to cure which defines the line dividing psychotherapy from psychoanalysis.

The analyst acts as the inner support of an intersubjective dynamic that keeps the questions from the patient about him or herself alive and leaves the listening ear of the analyst open or purified. So while it delimits a centre – what we have been looking for all this time with the question of standards – the centre is in fact an empty centre. This is different from the silence of an undisputed truth or the refuge of a refusal to justify one's actions that are a priori *tried and true* – what might characterise how contemporary analysis situates the analyst.[7] The analytic position is one the analyst does not identify with or take as equal to him or herself; it is merely a space occupied by the one who welcomes discourse, who supports a question but does not answer the question, leaving that answer to come from the patient. It involves a kind of radical openness at the point where one experiences a fundamental limit; in the case of the analyst the limits of love and knowledge. This opening is at once intimate and foreign, a wound and a cure. Lacan calls this 'extraterritoriality' and later names it 'extimacy', a neologism that combines 'exterior' and 'intimacy'. The unconscious is for each of us a kind of intimate exteriority, or exterior intimacy. As well, Lacan contrasts this aspect of the refuge that he calls ethical with the omnipotent refuge of ill-defined standards and formalistic control that characterise contemporary psychoanalysis. Further, the corrupt version of 'extraterritoriality' is one where psychoanalysis can appeal to other forms of knowledge, like science, for validation (especially today with the vogue of neuroscientific proof that acts, as Lacan sometimes called it, as an insurance policy), and then reject scientific standards when an appeal to the uniqueness of psychoanalysis suits them.[8] This is a refuge that is neither ethical nor rigorously scientific, but rather the means of further dissimulation.

Lacan turns to Edward Glover's 1954 article 'Therapeutic Criteria of Psycho-Analysis' in order to demonstrate this very crisis at work in the current theorisation of psycho-analytic criteria.[9] Quite uncharacteristically, Lacan almost always has positive things to say about Glover, whose rhetorical flair approximates Lacan's own, unlike most other dull and standard analytic writing. Glover's article is particularly bleak and vitriolic about the current state of psychoanalysis, no doubt part of the reason Lacan quotes it so extensively. Lacan uses Glover to show how little analysts agree on treatment criteria. In fact the most damning statement by Glover is that while analysts clearly do not practice or maintain the same standards, and the institutes are 'riven by differences' which lead to practices that must be as different as 'chalk from cheese', they put on a unified front, not only for the public, but in relation to one another: here there is a 'sedulously cultivated assumption that the participants in such discussions hold roughly the same views, speak the same technical language, follow identical systems . . . practice the same technical procedures, and obtain much the same results . . . which are held to be satisfactory. *Not one of these assumptions will bear close investigation.*'[10] Meanwhile, Glover continues, 'we have next to no information about the conduct of private analytic practice . . . we have no after-histories worth talking about. Certainly no record of failures. This lack of verifiable information, when added to the loose assumptions I have already set out, fosters the development of a psychoanalytic *mystique* which not only baffles investigation but blankets all healthy discussion.' The problem, seemingly, will only grow worse and worse, or, as Glover says, the criteria of psychoanalysis will become increasingly 'perfectionist, undefined, and uncontrolled'.[11]

Lacan takes up the charge here of a growing *mystique* as the effects of group psychology on psychoanalysis, where maintenance of standards is no longer about 'healthy discussion' or 'scientific' understanding, but falls more and more 'within the ambit of the groups interests' and power. 'What is at stake is thus less a standard, than standing.'[12] Lacan puts the nail in the coffin: what is meant by standard technique is simply what you have to do (or say you do) to be considered one of the group. In fact, Glover makes an important point in his article, one which goes unreferenced by Lacan, regarding allegiance to groups and its effects on psychoanalytic technique. Glover points out that we must include the psychoanalysis of the analyst as one of the technical modifications of psychoanalytic practice, for an analyst who comes from years and years of analysis practised with allegiance to a tradition of interpretation will not have the courage to confess the failure of his training and set about a sound analytical re-orientation: 'On the contrary he is much more likely to preserve his self-respect by maintaining a fanatical conviction on the special virtues of the tradition on which he has been nourished.'[13] What Glover is pointing out is that since interpretation seems governed by allegiance to one's group, and not necessarily based on some truth coming from the analysis, this will only strengthen group dynamics and fanaticism. Glover's conclusion to this important article is that the extension or delimitation of therapeutic criteria depends on the 'degree to which we can succeed in eliminating . . . the influence of a defensive, esoteric, but so far unconfessed mystique'. And, 'although elimination of the esoteric is supposed to be one of the tasks of training analysis there are in my view few signs that this important aim has so far been achieved'.[14] The negative institutional effects extend to the very core of psychoanalytic practice and the formation of the next generation of analysts. If what is transmitted is only some kind of group allegiance, some vampiric system of mimesis, then, as Freud must ask, 'Is that still psychoanalysis?'

One must see the discord of diverging theories as a coherent trajectory around a central axis, like the 'rigor with which the shrapnel of a projectile, in dispersing, maintains its ideal trajectory'.[15] Indeed, like an unfolding psychoanalysis, symptoms can mutate, get better or worse, go underground, and reappear. What is important is the direction of the treatment, what Lacan feels invariably underlies these changes. It is the analyst's job to have a sense of this direction as the one who directs the treatment. This is true for Lacan even when the analyst is not *directive* in his stance of general neutrality and adherence to the rules of free association. Can we do this work of finding the direction, the trajectory, with psychoanalysis as our subject? Psychoanalysis as our patient?

How does the analyst orient his patient? The patient must demand psychoanalysis from the analyst for it to properly begin! The patient must begin with a question, addressed to the analyst, with an implicit demand for psychoanalysis. This is one of the basic tenets of beginning a treatment and of Lacan's concept of preliminary sessions, which must bring a patient to this point for the psychoanalysis to properly begin. Often patients begin without really asking for an analysis, and may in fact come because their partner sent them, or because they want the analyst to make a symptom go away, but they have not asked a fundamental question, which inherently demands psychoanalysis. So, we are back again to the centre of analysis being the analyst put in the position to support the patient's coming to ask a question; the irony being that Glover stated that no questions are any longer really being asked . . . So, according to Lacan, no one is assuming the position of psychoanalyst any longer. Again we return to a question of the position an analyst occupies, but does not identify with, nor control. This is what gives the analyst their standing, and could begin to orient any question of standards. Nothing more, nothing less.

II

The threat that variation exacts on standard psychoanalysis (in the same measure that Lacan was perceived as such a threat) indicates that the existence of psychoanalysis is rather precarious and requires a 'real man' to maintain its pathway.[16] From now on in section II of Lacan's paper, the analyst who is called upon to shore up the profession will be referred to as 'the real man'. This is funny on a number of levels. The machismo of the 'real man' analyst will be a useful *a contrario* image for what Lacan would like to put forth. Also, that machismo is posited as a response to the feeling that one's identity is under threat, or simply, a response to ambiguity.

'The real man' is solicited to see what effect the ambiguities of psychoanalysis have on him in his role of maintaining its pathway. But if the question of the limit remains common, meaning the limited pathway he must travel in conducting a standard psychoanalytic treatment, it is because no one sees where the ambiguity ends, especially when the end of psychoanalysis remains ambiguous, no less what one does or why. Should 'the real man' spare himself the effort of having to define this endpoint? Well, Lacan says, the real man can take his word from the authorities who make it a rather confused affair, as we are about to see in Lacan's survey of the literature on termination. Or, paradoxically, he can rigorously misrecognise the endpoint by avoiding any experience of a limit, which nonetheless implies that he has registered its place.[17]

Lacan's comments about the forced choice presented to candidates in psychoanalytic training continues to this day, namely, between identifying with an established doctrine, and/or rigorously avoiding what is difficult in psychoanalysis. If what is difficult is being avoided – namely the questions that inevitably arise as one confronts something new in each patient – the analyst senses its existence in the act of avoidance, most likely, Lacan speculates, because they aren't provided with the tools to handle it, since they fall outside the purview of established standards. The literature on termination, no less technique, is still remarkably impoverished.[18]

This situation is what Lacan calls 'the bad faith of instituted practice' where one is duped by one's action more than performing any actions of real consequence.[19] I have often come across candidates in supervision who cling to their identifications with their previous supervisors to avoid the real confrontation in the treatment, in the transference. It is this rigorous avoidance, buttressed by the logic of identification, which I believe Lacan is speaking to.

What he calls the 'path of true humility' would require nothing less than a confrontation with the rather unbearable ambiguity of the psychoanalytic situation in and of itself, which isn't some special secret for initiates, but is within everyone's grasp: 'it is revealed in the question of what it means to speak, and one encounters it simply by welcoming discourse'.[20] What Lacan is pointing out is that the very premise of psychoanalysis – inviting someone to speak to you about him or herself – immediately erupts in unbearable ambiguity. Every analyst, no less any human being, understands the anxiety that makes its presence felt when solicited to speak about what is most intimate, to speak freely to another person. This is an ambiguity that resides in the very act of speaking and listening, not just in speaking to a psychoanalyst. So the analyst not only supports the patient's question about themselves, but also their speech.

If we 'mean to say' something, as in the colloquial phrase 'what I meant to say was', there is already a recognition of an ambiguity at the heart of speaking – what Lacan calls a 'double entendre' – that is up to the listener to hear and decide upon; whether the listener follows what this 'means to say' or what it does not say or does say in spite of what is meant.[21] Lacan is speaking to a fundamental division in the subject. We are not in control of our message. The act of speaking illuminates two different subjects: 1) the subject that says I, the subject that means to say, the subject of the statement, and, 2) the subject that is spoken of, what Lacan calls the subject of the enunciation, the subject that appears in a discourse. We might term the first the ego, and the second, the subject of the unconscious.[22] The more elusive 'subject of the unconscious' can be recognised by *both* the speaker and the listener, but requires attention to the beyond of what is intentionally trying to be conveyed.

A point often made is that this is not a theory of speech as *communication* which assumes a direct circuit from speaker to listener, from point A to point B and back. There is, for Lacan, a radical gap which necessitates a decision or choice about what to attend to. This asymmetrical structure is made all the more extreme by the rules of psychoanalysis, in particular the one rule given to patients, modelled on Freud's idea of free association: to speak without stopping, without holding anything back, without regard for rationality, coherence, politeness or shamefulness.[23] As the analysis proceeds, by speaking and speaking and speaking, meaning flies out from underneath intention. At some point, Lacan imagines, the analyst might pin his hopes on the patients finally finding themselves equal to what they were saying. What is said and the act of saying, could join together in a great unity, with the force of revelation.

The analyst must retain 'complete responsibility' in his position as listener, and, what's more, he solicited this responsibility when he invited the patient to speak, something that acts as 'a secret summons' that will not be dismissed even if the analyst remains silent.[24] Speaking and listening is the engine of the transference, and nothing more. It is not some mysterious meta-psychological substance that oozes from the unconscious. It is a factor of language. Lacan returns us here to a question of ethics, pointing to the weight of welcoming words and the responsibility of the analyst facing this deep division in the subject and the ambiguity of speech that will *never* be resolved, either by the analyst or by the patient, whatever fantasy we might have about it. Again, Lacan is defining something absolutely critical to how he views the analytic position, not as a set of procedures or some mystical property of psychoanalysis, but as the pathway initiated by a 'talking' therapy.

It is at this point that he will now turn to how 'contemporary psychoanalysis' deals with interpretation, and he will spare no one.[25] Lacan begins by pointing out how uneasy analysts seem in the face of defining interpretation, that their theories are awkward and formless. It is often recommended that analysts not 'interpret' for many, many years into an analysis. While this is true for Lacanians who tend to avoid 'meaningful' interpretations, playing with speech that is more ambiguous or oracular, waiting for the analysand to find their way with meaning, many of the other schools veer away from interpretation in favour of other techniques like confrontation, explanation, insight, mirroring, holding, all of which move further and further from speech and language while keeping to the idea of conveying 'meaning' both in what needs to be said to the patient (explanation, confrontation), or not said but done for the patient's benefit (mirroring, holding). The vogue for analysing counter-transference, rather than interpreting transference – meaning the analyst thinks about his own feeling and ideas about a patient rather than responding interpretively to what a patient has said – is just one more move away from the one action an analyst is to take, namely, for Lacan, to respond to what a patient has literally said in a way that opens a new truth. Lacan here quips that it's a good thing the students of 'the real man' are too ashamed to make him explain what they are supposed to be doing.[26]

Lacan goes on to the question of the analysis of the resistances, which had come to replace the classical idea of interpretation 'of the material', as ego-psychology gained dominance with Anna Freud in London and then with émigré analysts in the United States.[27] The proof for the value of interpreting resistance is that it produces new material.[28] For example, a

classical resistance interpretation will either point to a break
in free association, a lack or point of stoppage – 'You are
reluctant to speak today', 'You did not associate to the dream
you mentioned in passing' – or it will specifically address
a refusal to speak about some material – 'You do not want
to address my upcoming vacation', 'You never say anything
about your father when you speak of your parents' divorce',
and so on. The patient will then speak to what they were previously resistant to – the dream, the vacation, the father – and
then that material can be interpreted. Lacan points out that
there is still a question here, because if the analyst then goes
on to 'interpret the material', which is what he was supposed
to do in the first place and is the focus of Freudian technique,
'will we be justified in wondering whether the term "interpretation" has the same meaning at these two different points in
time', meaning interpreting from the get-go or interpreting
after an interpretation of the resistances.[29] This is the crux of
Lacan's question to the justification for this shift in technique:
if you have set up the analysis as interpreting the resistances,
or its later incarnation as defence interpretation, and only
afterwards interpreting the material (be it an interpretation
of fantasy, sexuality, Oedipus, etc.), does the interpretation of
resistance fundamentally alter the material to be interpreted?
And further, does this shift in technique create other effects
in the field of psychoanalysis as a whole? What happens when
the psychoanalyst is in the position to constantly know what
the analysand isn't, and should be, speaking about? As the
focus shifts towards analysis of resistance as standard technique, there will be major ramifications.

Lacan points out that Freud spoke of resistance as early
as 1895, locating resistance in the verbalisation of chains of
speech or interconnected units composed of pieces of memories, things heard and seen, all wrapped around a core trauma.[30] This is how Freud conceptualised both the difficulty
patients had speaking about the origin of their symptoms, as
well as why they often veered away from it onto seemingly

unconnected associations. Seeing how the patient moved from one set of thoughts to another, which seemed unrelated but eventually could be brought into line with the original repressed or resisted thoughts, was the beginning of the creation of the technique of free association. In this early model there is both resistance at work in a chain and between chains, all of which bend around a pathogenic nucleus or what Lacan would later call the traumatic 'Real'. The analyst can gauge how close or distant he is to this nucleus by virtue of the intensity of this resistance. Resistance in a chain is different from that between chains to the extent that the first involves moving through a series of related associations that form one articulated chain or thought, whereas moving between chains implies moving closer to the traumatic core, getting closer to the kernel of truth. The emphasis for Lacan in this model of resistance is a technique that looks at the very text of what a patient comes to say, hearing elusions, distortions, gaps, syncopes and holes in the process of association.

As attention to language and the constituting subject of the unconscious are sacrificed, the more nuanced Freudian concept of unconscious resistance as the logical network of chains of signifiers that appear in the approach to the traumatic pathogenic nucleus will be obscured, confused, and finally replaced by the idea of ego defence. The constant trope of ego-psychology was that analysis needed to attack the defences of the ego (which paradoxically strengthens weak egos) and adapt the patient to reality through bringing about more rational compromise formations (symptomatic compromises between the drive, reality and super-ego). For Lacan this goal or endpoint of treatment is not psychoanalytic, it is ideological and based on a world-view, that of 1950s American expansionist capitalism or a 'theology of free enterprise'. The 'real man's' maintenance of the pathway of psychoanalysis begins to look more and more like the pathway of an attack on the patient in the name of a certain vision or image that becomes the therapeutic ideal. Lacan thought the new psychoanalytic ideal of health was one modelled on the aggressiveness of the American lawyer. Just enough to get what he wants. Libido, or desire, falls by the wayside.[31] (As an aside, it's interesting to fast-forward to 2004 when Peter Fonagy and Mary Target, the chief executives of the Anna Freud Centre, declare that sex needs to be put back into psychoanalysis.)[32]

III

Lacan begins section III of the paper more or less asking how anyone can see the ego as the point of strength for the analyst.[33] The good or strong ego is at stake everywhere in the additions to classical technique from the healing power of empathy, to the importance of assessment, and the use value of counter-transference analysis. In each of these cases the ego is put forward as the subject's collateral or safety, and, for Lacan, this is no foundation upon which to build oneself or psychoanalysis.[34] In Freud's 'Analysis Terminable and Interminable' (1937), Lacan points out that Freud is abundantly clear on this topic: 'analysts in their own personalities have not invariably come up to the standard of psychical normality to which they wish to educate their patients'.[35] The analyst's ego is not a model of health or normality, it is not the standard in 'standard treatment', nor the type in a 'typical psychoanalysis'.

To demand such an image from the analyst only adds to the weight that Sándor Ferenczi acknowledges as the extreme and ongoing difficulties that the analyst faces in his task as analyst: during long hours of listening to patients, analysts must split themselves between a focus on the patient, self-control, and intellectual activity; they cannot give free play to narcissism or egoism, and even in fantasy, only very minimally.[36] There isn't much in everyday life that makes these kinds of demands; Ferenczi had written to Freud mentioning the idea of the analyst's ongoing mental 'hygiene'.[37] Though Ferenczi ultimately considered this hygiene inadequate and never wrote the paper he wanted to about it, aren't these extreme constraints the reason that the analyst's analysis is so crucial? What the analyst must bring about in himself in order to endure the task of being a psychoanalyst seems to Lacan not to be a strengthening of the ego, but rather its effacing.[38] We efface our egos in order to give way to the patient and their 'subject-point' of interpretation. This can only take place on the basis of the analyst's personal analysis, *especially its end.* We might recall that Glover stated that personal analysis seems to have failed to bring anything about except fanaticism and mystification, and that in Lacan's perusal of the literature, psychoanalysis is unable to conceptualise its end. If you don't know where you are going, how are you going to get there? This confusion continues unabated until the answer 'identification with the analyst's ego' becomes the *raison d'être* for all schools, chalk and cheese, in mid-century psychoanalysis. 'Where' then 'is the end of analysis as far as the ego is concerned?' Lacan asks.[39]

Wilhelm Reich seems an apt figure for Lacan to bring in here because his 1933 book *Character Analysis* laid the groundwork for ego-psychology and provides a kind of extreme example of where this thought may take one, with Reich moving on to analysis of the body without the use of language or talking, his focus on orgastic potency and the control of what he called Orgone energy through devices that he built, a belief in militant communism, and eventually, a breakdown into paranoid delusion.[40] Lacan says that Reich's theories force us to look closely at how the tensions that analysis creates and seeks to resolve are characterised, in particular as one symptomatises personality:

> The whole theory that Reich provides of it is based on the idea that these structures are a defense by the individual against the orgasmic effusion whose primacy in

lived experience can alone ensure its harmony. The extremes this idea led him to are well known – they went so far as to get him ousted by the analytic community. But, in ousting him not unjustifiably, no one ever really knew how to formulate why Reich was wrong.[41]

Lacan is beginning his elucidation of why Reich was wrong by pointing out that if the personality is a symptom, defensively structured like armour that the subject carries around, this armour has significance.[42] It is not simply there to be attacked to get to the thing. The armour is actually an armorial, a coat of arms, with traces of a subject's history and pre-history, namely, what the subject inherits.

The armour as signifier, not the signification of armour, is what the work of analysis is focused on for Lacan: unravelling one's history through signifiers, the weight of past identifications, one's desire as desire of the Other, intergenerational transmission of trauma, and finally, the mark as the mark of death and finitude. Reich's refusal of the death drive as the most radical psychoanalytic discovery is what Lacan insinuates forces Reich to go too far, to pursue the Thing, *jouissance* itself![43] Consider Reich's Orgone theory: achieving absolute 'orgastic potential' was destined to become more and more literal, an imaginary object that one must have full access to and control over (with Orgone boxes and machines that tried to capture its energy in the atmosphere), eventually seen as access to God or Godlikeness. So while Reich refuses the death drive, his work, for Lacan, is the death drive incarnate; or, to put it another way, this is the ideal precisely as death-driven. While Lacan does eventually speak about mystical *jouissance*, it is not something we ever have controlled access to. It will always be Other, and always only appear through a representational system. Surface is depth. Reich's stance, in the end, is fundamentally paranoid – consolidating and personifying the position of the Other – which Lacan linked early on in the mirror stage to both the mania of the ego and the

image of mastery as absolute knowledge. Reich's life ended in
actual persecution by the law in 1956 – a fate brought down
on many paranoiacs – and his death in prison in 1957. 'Reich's
error can be explained by his deliberate refusal of the signification that is tied to the death instinct, which was introduced
by Freud at the height of his conceptual powers, and which
is, as we know, the touchstone of the mediocrity of analysts,
whether they reject it or disfigure it.'[44]

Having deconstructed Reich, Lacan goes on to elaborate his view of the ego, reviewing his work on the mirror stage. First of all, he says, if we follow neurosis and the
structure of desire, we do not find some Valhalla of orgasmic
energy and total satisfaction, we do not find some original
naturalistic relation to sex and pleasure, that had merely
been distorted by neurosis, but something else.[45] What we
glean from analysis is something about the structure of
desire and the twisted development of the human personality: the alienation of desire, the desire for desire, the desire
for recognition, all of which are modulated and structured
through the vicissitudes of sexuality in all the forms of sexual perversion that Freud chronicled in his *Three Essays on
the Theory of Sexuality* (1905). When we looks closely at sexual perversions we find both the dominance of narcissism
and the precariousness of desire, the splitting of the subject into 'existence and facticity' (subject, object and Other,
contained in the positions laid out in a perverse fantasy,
for example the aggressor, the victim and the witness), and,
finally, the ambivalence that rests on passionate love linked
to the ego-ideal and the hate that follows from such inevitable dependence on others.[46] For Lacan, in these early works
of Freud we have some of the most important tools at our
disposal for clinical understanding, especially regarding the
structure of symptoms and fantasy. We can see the multiple
positions unconsciously assumed by the patient, the place
where desire and symptom run up against one another, and,
in following the vicissitudes of sexuality, we will find what

has historically marked a subject.

Lacan links these findings not only to Freud's *Group Psychology and the Analysis of the Ego* from 1921, but eventually to *Civilization and Its Discontents* from 1930.[47] The ego, far from being the object of aversion, as Anna Freud states in her prophetic sinister music, is everywhere in Freud during this period. If we turn from sexuality to the question of aggression, what we see in Freud's work from this period is that it has nothing to do with some natural aggression linked to Darwinian survival and evolution but what Lacan calls our 'dehiscence from natural harmony':

> The rending of the subject from himself, a rending whose primordial moment comes when the sight of the other's image, apprehended by him as a unified whole, anticipates his sense that he lacks motor co-ordination, this image retroactively structuring this lack of motor co-ordination in images of fragmentation . . . It is thus at the heart of experiences of bearing and intimidation during the first years of life that the individual is introduced to the mirage of mastery of his functions, in which his subjectivity will remain split, and whose imaginary formation, naively objectified by psychologists as the ego's synthetic function, manifests instead the condition that introduces him to the alienating master/slave dialectic.[48]

This is man's 'fruitful illness', his Hegelian 'happy fault', namely his being divided from himself, in the case of Freud conscious and unconscious, or for Hegel the divide between essence and appearance, which Hegel links to the fall of man and original sin.[49] Lacan shows how man's relation to the image, its mark, introduces him to the vicissitudes of both life and death specific to the human being who apprehends himself, outside himself, in an image. The ego, for Lacan, is always only half the subject, and represents a point of loss, a gap, a rending in human development, what Freud always indicated with the idea of the lost object. It is no wonder that the subject clings to the image as a place where he attempts to recognise himself – *There I am!* But this manoeuvre only divides the subject rather than uniting him with himself. Like with the earlier discussion of speech, this division cannot be overcome.[50] Psychoanalytic theory seems to have come to ignore this basic Freudian truth.

What does this mean for technique? Lacan agrees that analysis brings the narcissistic mirage into full being in the regression of treatment, in particular as a demand for recognition by the analyst.[51] How does the analyst respond to this? On the one hand, response can elicit a powerful transference love whose presence and passion for presence dominates the analysis. Love for the analyst and the analyst's self-love are in a *danse macabre* as the patient's idealisation meets with the analyst's narcissism. Analysis becomes interminable. On the other hand, a lack of response often provokes the aggression and hatred of a negative transference. The analyst's aggressive interpretations are met with aggression by the patient *ad infinitum*. Analysis is often prematurely terminated. What the analyst knows less well, Lacan says, is that 'what he says in his response is less important here than the place from which he responds'.[52]

Lacan will come back to this at the end of this section, but it is probably one of his most important remarks – in this section certainly, but perhaps in the entire paper. It goes back to the question of the position of the analyst. Here, he is linking the place from which the analyst responds to this question of death, the position of the analyst being to maintain the presence of death in a refusal of closure, the only master in the game being death. The analyst will not play the master. Any figure of mastery other than death will lead to a closure of the unconscious. Therefore 'the subjectification of death' is linked, for the first time, to the psychoanalytic cure.[53] It is a very Heideggerian rendering of the project of analysis, something that would wane over time in Lacan's work. Nevertheless, the import of the structure of death as the mediating term retains its centrality through to the end of Lacan's teaching. The reason to bring these remarks forward at this point is because Lacan is here synthesising the co-ordinates of the dilemmas of the ego in psychoanalysis. If the analyst increasingly 'falls under the sway of the illusions of his own ego', where the 'shaping of the subject by the analyst's ego serves merely as an excuse for the analyst's narcissism', the question is, how does death intervene in order to avoid this distortion of psychoanalytic treatment?[54]

There is no reality except for the reality of death for Lacan. This is crucial. It is death, not reality. This extreme 'subjectification' of death is the only way that an analyst can then bring another to this ecstatic limit of the self. No one is a master when death takes its proper place, and if this doesn't wipe out knowledge altogether (perhaps in an elevation of non-knowledge), knowledge at least loses its imaginary power of fascination. Knowledge as a form of mastery is not the economy that psychoanalysis will deal in. The analyst is only the subject *supposed* to know. 'Thus he [the analyst] can now respond to the subject from the place he wants to respond from.'[55] It is this shift from knowing to supposed knowing that provides the place from which the analyst can respond to his patient's desire for recognition. It is from this place that technique will take its bearings.

'This brings us to the following question: What must the analyst know in analysis?'[56] Lacan wonders what kind of knowledge is knowledge of death and what death does to knowledge. Who wants to have anything to do with this necrophiliac version of psychoanalysis? Even if one might characterise the analyst as a kind of death-like creature – silently expectant, passive, indifferent, blank, maybe even dumb – and this allows the analyst to subordinate himself to the subject's truth, Lacan's vision is more radical than what can look like a kind of psychoanalytic posturing. How does this confrontation with death transform the analyst to take on the difficulties of day in, day out analytic work? Might we imagine that after the analyst's analysis, he or she might want nothing to do with analysis any longer? That the analyst might want to get on with life rather than turn right back around and help others in this death-work? This raises fascinating questions concerning the masochism of the analyst, how a cure affects the desire of the analyst to be an analyst, why the possibility of not wanting to be an analyst must be part of any training and its end, and finally what termination means about the position the analyst is able to occupy. Lacan sometimes characterised this as the confrontation with the impossible, which took on many guises throughout his lifetime: from the figure of death, to castration, the shattering of the Real, to his iteration on there being no Other of the Other, no final judgement, no Woman, no sexual relationship, to his late work on the limits of love and knowledge, and the subjective destitution of the psychoanalytic cure. The analyst falls as an object of desire at the end of treatment, and, sometimes, they are even flushed away like a piece of shit.

IV

The problem of the ego, increasingly highlighted by Lacan's paper, in the end proves critical to the cure in the same manner in which the repetition compulsion becomes repetition in the transference, in order to open out in both remembering and working-through. So, far from the ego being simply an obstacle, Lacan now makes the claim that just because it belongs to the imaginary 'does not mean that it is illusory'. In fact, if one looks at imaginary numbers in mathematics, or an ideal point in geometry, it acts as 'the pivotal point of transformation', a nodal point in a 'convergence' of forms and figures, determined *by* reality, not against it.[57]

It seems clear, Lacan conjectures, that while the analyst

does not know what he is doing, and changes 'nothing in "real-ity"', still psychoanalysis 'changes everything for the subject'. Notions like 'distortion of reality', 'wishful thinking' or 'magi-cal thinking', as something to be corrected by analysis, are not at the core of transformation for Lacan, they are simply an 'excuse for ignorance'.[58] Terms like 'distortion' or 'wish' have proven themselves in the history of the psychoanalytic liter-ature to be indices of the (male) analyst's imaginary power – his knowledge considered as a privileged point – exploiting the naive faith of the patient who sees him as a man 'not like the others'.[59] What reality? Or rather, whose? Once we are ask-ing a question of who determined the outlines of a supposed reality, namely the construction of a fantasy around a certain ideal, we are closer to the nodal ideal point of any imaginary form. Lacan's infamous example of this can be found in his seminar 'The Logic of Fantasy' (1966–67) with its reading of Freud's 'A Child Is Being Beaten' (1919), where in the imag-inary masturbatory scene of a father figure beating many children there is often a hidden instrument – be it a horse-whip, or an engraved paddle, or an ivory cane – that is full of significance. The subject is indicated by this ideal point, this instrument, which is often saturated by symbolic content if one looks closely at the fantasy, something that itself is hid-den by the *jouissance* engendered by the scene.[60]

Lacan breaks off this discussion suddenly and returns to his claim that what the analyst does is support speech, ask-ing the question: *What is speech?* Lacan is immediately in the contradictory, somewhat tautological position of explaining what speech is, with speech, and with having to articulate the meaning of meaning. Speech is not reducible to mean-ing, and meaning is not reducible to speech. However, speech does 'give meaning its medium in the symbol that speech incarnates through its act . . . it is thus an act and, as such, pre-supposes a subject'. When speech functions as an act, when it deploys meaning by summoning the symbolic, it brings a subject into being. Lacan brings up the declaration, 'You are my master', which signifies 'I am your disciple'.[61] Nevertheless, this can be heard by the listener in two ways: as a statement about the relationship between speaker and listener, or as a description. The speech act on the side of the subject is what Lacan will call 'true speech', while 'true discourse' is based in knowledge as 'correspondence to the thing'; in other words, speech that says 'I' and speech that says 'that'. Speech that says 'I' constitutes a truth the less it is based on true discourse and the more it is based on a subject's investment in and recognition of their own being. True discourse is constituted as knowledge of reality, outside of the intersubjective dimension. The ego position of the analyst or analysand is often an investment in true discourse at the expense of true speech. *That's the way it is*, split off from its other half, *because that's the way I say it is.*

Lacan says that true discourse accuses true speech of lying, since it points to the promissory nature of any declaration; true speech pledges a future that belongs to no one. Ambiguity is always present, since the future outruns the speaking person in question, who is always 'outstripped'. When someone says, 'I love you', the retort is often, as the famous song goes, 'And what about tomorrow?' One has to say 'I love you' again and again and again. Nevertheless, on the side of true speech, it questions true discourse as to what it signifies, since one signification leads to another to another.[62] 'What do you mean when you say you love me?' 'What do you love about me?' 'When did you decide you loved me?', and so on. As lover's discourse shows us, it cannot catch up to the thing. The unending questions of children – 'Why is the sky blue? What is air? Who made air? What is time? How do you know?', and so on – often lead back to an ur-question regarding why the parent is answering the child's questions to begin with, and the position they occupy as the one who supposedly knows. The child demands an answer on the level of true speech, not true discourse, its forgotten or obscured other half.

How does this support of authentic speech happen? Lacan begins with a bleak pronouncement: authentic speech is forbidden to the analysand except in rare moments of one's existence – hence the need for psychoanalysis. Nevertheless, truth speaks and can be read in 'all the levels at which it [speech] has shaped him'. Lacan once again grounds being through an intersubjective foundation at the level of speech, a foundation that can be read by the psychoanalyst. Lacan becomes very theoretical at this point. He says that what the analyst must do is 'silence the intermediate discourse in himself in order to open himself up to the chain of true speech, that he can interpolate his revelatory interpretation'.[63] The best way to understand this cryptic statement is to turn to his reading of Freud's case of the Rat Man.[64]

Lacan's claim is that Freud solves the riddle of the Rat Man's obsessional neurosis in opening himself up to a 'word chain' that unpacks the Rat Man's history, providing 'the meaning by which we can understand the simulacrum of redemption that the subject foments to the point of delusion in the course of the great obsessive trance that leads him to ask for Freud's help'.[65] As noted previously, the Rat Man came to Freud because he couldn't stop thinking of a rat torture (described to him by his captain in the army) being performed on his father and his own lover if he wasn't able to return the money that he'd borrowed from another soldier to pay for a new pair of glasses to replace those he'd lost. Through a series of tricks of obsessional logic, he landed himself with an impossible duty to pay back Lieutenant A by paying back Lieutenant B. His father was dead, which somehow didn't prevent the possibility of rat torture in the afterlife. Following the logic of this delusional 'simulacra' of redemption, Freud traced the word *Raten* ('rats') to *Ratten* ('instalments') through a series of associations circling around an infamous unpaid gambling debt of the Rat Man's father's from his days in the army, which had led to his discharge. The unconscious accusation concerned a monetary-characterological problem of his father, which, in the long run, led to his marrying the Rat Man's mother for money, and not the woman he loved. This cast a shadow over the whole of his parent's marriage, and, at the point that the Rat Man fell ill, his mother was hypocritically asking the Rat Man to make a similar 'calculation' in his choice of a wife.[66] In other words, she was asking him to marry a woman for her wealth and not the one he loved, forcing the Rat Man into a fate similar to his parents in the model of a reverse Oedipus complex. Lacan points out that in his symptom, the Rat Man unites the real Oedipal couple, his father and the lover, show-ing his own desire to marry the woman he loves and not fol-low his mother's ultimatum and repeat his family history.

This chain, unpacked by Freud, is in fact not made up of 'pure events (all of which had, in any case, occurred prior to the subject's birth), but rather of a failure (which was perhaps the most serious because it was the most subtle)'.[67] Questions of trauma and truth still haunt the history of psychoanalysis. The Rat Man is witness to a truth about his family, a truth that precedes his very birth, leaving its stamp on his life. We are back to the analysis of Reich's armour as an armorial. The Rat Man's coat of arms would have a rat and money inscribed on it in the section that depicts the history of marriage in this family. As well, this is the ideal point of the imaginary that is subverted in a reading of its signification. In pointing out that the Rat Man is more a witness than a legatee, Lacan indicates that analysis gives him back a choice regarding this legacy; in other words, the Rat Man is brought to a point where he can live up to his truth. This nodal point acts like a symbolic debt, meaning something owned and assumed, ultimately unfulfillable, so lived with, rather than a real debt, which can be paid off, like the money for his glasses.[68] In fact, the Rat Man went on to marry the woman he loved – sadly just before dying in the war.

Perhaps most important with regard to technique, Lacan says that Freud was able to touch on this crucial point because a 'similar suggestion' had been made to Freud himself by his

family and proved critical in his self-analysis.[69] Lacan conjectures that if Freud had not analysed his relationship to money
as it circulated in his family mythology, he might have missed
it in the Rat Man. While the effects of Freud's narcissism in his
clinical work are a subject of much investigation, especially
in the Dora case, still, Lacan says, 'the dazzling comprehen-
sion Freud demonstrates . . . allows us to see that, in the lofty
heights of his final doctrinal constructions, the paths of being
were cleared for him'.[70] In other words, Freud's self-analysis
– as a clearing of being, or bringing being into a clearing (to
put it in Heideggerian terms) – worked, and it is precisely this
which allowed Freud to open himself to the linguistic chain
and read the Rat Man's story. While this of course points to
the importance of reading Freud's cases closely, it also brings
us to our last stop in the discussion of the analyst's knowledge.

Psychoanalytic training, Lacan says, is not about the
transmission of a set body of knowledge.[71] 'The positive fruit
of the revelation of ignorance is non-knowledge, which is
not a negation of knowledge, but rather its most elaborate
form. The candidate's training cannot be completed without some action on the part of the master or masters who
train him in this non-knowledge – failing which he will never
be anything more than a robotic analyst.'[72] An experience of
non-knowledge, as the most elaborate form of knowledge,
is critical to the formation of a psychoanalyst. Whether this
is something about the candidate's experience in analysis or
supervision, or an experience with teachers who know not
to fetishise knowledge, who proceed Socrates-like, a revelatory encounter with ignorance is essential. Most of the
knowledge that analysis has accumulated, Lacan posits, as a
'natural history of the forms of desire's capture and even of
the subject's identifications' that had never before been this
rigorously catalogued, is not of use to him in his action as
analyst.[73] While depicting the capture of desire in true discourse is notoriously difficult – since it is about the truth
of illusion and the limits of illusion, which are never stable

– nonetheless, this is of little help to the analyst since it concerns the deposit and not the mainspring.[74] In other words, it does not concern what generates the world of the imaginary, what constructs the veil.

Psychoanalysis, for Lacan, is best when subordinated to its unique purpose, which is a consideration of what is most particular about a subject. The universal 'wisdom' of science or cultural morality has little place in this ethic of the particular. What is required is not-knowing. What Freud says about psychoanalysis as a science, Lacan says, is that it is a science that puts itself in question with every new case.[75] Every case should bring what psychoanalysis thinks it knows into question. This dictum clearly indicates for Lacan the path that training should follow: in other words, pre-digested knowledge will be of no help when analysing a case. In fact, the analyst cannot analyse unless he 'recognizes in his knowledge the symptom of his own ignorance'. The desire to know is a symptom, maybe even *the* symptom, and must be treated like the neurotic's desire to love, which is what the 'best analytic writers' point to when they say that the reasons one wants to be an analyst must, above all, be analysed.[76]

Lacan refers the reader in a footnote to Maxwell Gitelson's 1954 article 'Therapeutic Problems in the Analysis of the "Normal" Candidate' – a now legendary paper – where he specifically takes up the challenge of Robert P. Knight's address, and the new ecology of candidates. Gitelson says that their professionalism is the first line of an intellectual defence, that the image of authority is now psychoanalysis itself, which makes it hard to analyse even in cases where candidates 'sincerely affirm their intellectual acceptance of analysis', and their normalcy works as a denial of the unconscious, especially in their phallic ambition, which is an oral substitute and defence against regression. They thus have great difficulty in 'surrendering' to the uncertain gratification and postponed solutions demanded by analysis, while the current analytic training system fosters these defensive solutions, rather than working against them, especially in its system of codified knowledge. This is especially true when the analysis of candidates, the so-called 'training analysis', is seen as a learning process distinct from therapy or regular analysis, in other words, as dealing in knowledge as though between a teacher and a student. To play the student (in line with eventually being the teacher-analyst) is a fantastic – or perhaps better, phantasmatic – obstacle seen at the very core of the decision to become an analyst. If the institution supports this phantasm, isn't the pathway of psychoanalysis lost?[77]

And so we come back to the 'closing'-up of the unconscious predicted by Freud in the 1920s as the turning point of analytic technique, linked by him to the potential effects of analysis becoming more widespread. 'Indeed the unconscious shuts down in so far as the analyst no longer "supports speech", because he already knows or thinks he knows what speech has to say'.[78] The patient cannot recognise his truth in what the analyst says, since it does not have the structure of truth as revelation, namely as the encounter with something new and absolutely specific to the patient. For Lacan, we can only listen to and speak through the unique signifiers at play in a case if we silence conscious knowledge and give not only the patient's unconscious voice, but also our own. This returns us to Lacan's question about the Being of the analyst and how Being and desire structure one's role as analyst and the position of the analyst: 'the analyst must know, better than anyone else, that he can only be himself in his speech'.[79]

Interpretation must be as surprising to the analyst as it is to the patient, as if what the analyst said literally fell out of the analyst's mouth. All of Lacan's emphasis on oracular speech finds resonance here, but with the added element of a lack of knowledge or intention. He can't just speak oracularly. His speech takes on the co-ordinates of an oracle, since it comes from elsewhere. The analyst will re-discover his own truth, in a new form, in every case. This real avowal in relation to the truth, by the analyst, the use of his being which acts even in silence, allows the patient to find his 'own desire' *in* the analyst in accordance with the laws of speech. While this might seem in danger of being nothing more than a narcissistic identification on the part of the analyst, it is the maintenance of Being on the level of the truth of speech that prevents it from being thus.[80] Lacan points out that narcissism is always the rejection of the commandments of speech (which he has been at great pains to show us throughout this paper) and one would see in an analysis of this nature the ferocious reign of the super-ego opened up by this solidification of the imaginary.

I have often been a patient's second (or third, or fourth) therapist; and while some symptoms might have resolved, their super-ego is as harsh as ever, especially in their discourse about themselves as symptomatic – *I have such and such problem, and it's for this and that reason.* They are thoroughly objectified. In Lacan's late paper 'L'Étourdit' (1973) he addresses the fantasy of final judgement, in other words the dictates of the super-ego, encountered as a kind of vanishing point in an analysis. The subject is the one that always vanishes and no judgement – usually partaking of the good/bad variety – can stabilise the subject. This instability, this vanishing act, is preferable to the avid stability of an objectified self. The subversion of the super-ego in the direction of this vanishing is necessary on an institutional level, Lacan claims, if psychoanalysis is going to function as such. In 'Variations on the Standard Treatment' that vanishing must take place on the plane of knowledge. So here we have the bi-directional co-ordinates of treatment: speech and Being on the one hand, and the imaginary and the super-ego on the other.

Lacan enters into one last parody of the modern-day analyst.[81] Here the analysand in training analysis confirms his knowledge of his Oedipal problems by confessing that he is in love with the woman who opens the door to his sessions, whom he believes is his analyst's wife. Lacan's quip here is that this titillating fantasy is just conformism and is hardly a lived knowledge of Oedipus, which in any case, would strip him entirely of this fancy when all is said and done, since Oedipus leads one through the narrow straits of castration. As Lacan said of Oedipus, 'it is not the scales that fell from his eyes, as if he could finally see, but his eyes that fell from him like scales'. What will happen, Lacan asks, when we ask this little chap who proves to be nothing other than 'a follower whose head is full of idle gossip' to add his 'two cents' worth to the question of variations in treatment?'[82] Brutal! The analyst has no standard by which to judge a variation, having discovered nothing but his own conformity in his analysis! And the hushed conditions surrounding training analysis (and which continue to this day) must not drive ideas concerning the means and ends of psychoanalytic treatment further into the shadows. 'A hundred mediocre psychoanalysts do not advance analytic knowledge one iota.'[83]

For Lacan, analysis must rectify one's relationship to desire. There is nothing but the desire for analysis, for the psychoanalysis to carry on, for the psychoanalysis to be psychoanalysis and not something else; purified, as he said in the very beginning, in its means and ends. Only then, he says, will we understand the extreme discretion of Freud when he says of 'standard treatment' that 'I must however make it clear that what I am asserting is that this technique is the only one suited to my individuality; I do not venture to deny that a physician quite differently constituted might find himself driven to adopt a different attitude to his patients and to the task before him.'[84] Of course Lacan points out that this is not a sign of Freud's profound modesty – some sort of idealisation of Freud that masks profound aggression – but rather a truth about the analyst's relation to knowledge. The analyst must know that he cannot proceed by way of mimicry of Freud, which in any case would only be formalistic, but rather finds his scale of measurement along the path of non-knowledge. To take this one step further, Lacan here implies that every analyst must reinvent psychoanalysis, must invent his own being and attitude and way as an analyst, and that Freud leaves this open; demands it, even. So, in a way, the 'standard treatment' decrees variation, this individual variation as invention of oneself as an analyst. Lacan ends by saying you can only be your own being, no doubt best done in speech, personal variation, style; and if you haven't encountered this necessity by the time you make your way into the analyst's chair, he grimly states, you will be lost and you will always be lost. How else can one make their way with the unconscious?

Part 3

The Cure Solidifies Nothing

Death Drive

A few months ago I had a dream that I was in a second-hand bookshop and found a book called *The Desiccation* – or maybe it was *The Decimation* – *of Coral*, a kind of almanac documenting where coral is dying or dead, showing how it is going extinct. As I flipped through the pages, I was stunned to find a drawing or game written in the margin which I recognised as my own, that I had made with a friend, something like a tic-tac-toe, noughts and crosses. His name, which begins with C and was indicated by this letter, was crossed out and replaced with the letter K, indicating someone else. In real life, C and K had had a disagreement and it was as if to say that K had won, that K was erasing – had decimated – C. The dream ended with an air of melancholia around the zero-sum game, though there was a lining of surprise that counteracted its force, as if to stop just shy of melancholia's certainty; I felt stunned at having found something of myself in this book which had drawn my attention unwittingly, and this surprise lifted the tense air.

Why did I find this book in order to find this image from my past? The dream was prefaced in reality by a series of gifts: I had bought a coral bracelet for another 'C' friend. We had found ourselves at some distance from one another lately. I loved this bracelet and had wanted it for myself and half regretted giving it to her. Later I would buy coral earrings for myself, a replacement that I recognised as barely sufficing, which I then lost twice.

In form, the dream plays with the hard and soft sounds associated with C, with C sounding like a K, and with C sounding like an S, as in 'desiccation' or 'decimation'. Importantly, the relationship is asymmetrical: C is an unreliable letter, phonetically sounding like other letters, bleeding into them or acting in silence, while K sounds like a K, holding its ground. On the evening of the dream I had watched Chris Marker's *La Jetée*, of which the dream is an interpretation: every investigation of time leads you to find yourself dying or already dead. It was also at this time that Louis CK had issued an apology for getting his dick out, which I had spoken of with others – was the apology sincere or not? C had told me that it was just CK getting his dick out again, this time it was his final *coup de grace*.

The dream itself was a prelude to a second dream, a nightmare, and a very violent one, that seemed to mark a point where a lot of things could be undone for me for a while. I'm interested in both dreams since the one acts as a signpost before a painful period of unbinding – interested in the attempt to find a letter, C-K, which is haunted by a negativity that increasingly manifests itself. The zero-sum game between C and K (one that indeed haunts all the relationships evoked by the dream) rears its head, pointing to the force of negation and erasure; while the dream attempts to find a point of minimal difference, C vs K, as the instability of the C phonetically bleeding into K threatens the very stability sought.

K keeps erasing C, even as the dream attempts to contain the difference, seen in the repeated iterations of these two figures. Does this structure begin to give representation to the loss that haunts the dream and animates its desire? Does it bring the negative into the foreground, marking the necessity for exchange in an asymmetry between partners? Or, does this attempt slide into the gap upon which it is constructed, eventually opening onto violence, anxiety, short-circuiting as a nightmare – too much on the side of the death drive? The nightmare is the negative underside of all love: not necessarily hate (though that is there), but the negativity implied by the loss (desiccation and decimation) that formed the desire and address in the first place.

It is at the place of this address that I believe that what threatens to come undone completely can find a response from the analyst, and, perhaps for many, only from an analyst – this is where the real threat is emanating from for you, signalled by these letters.

I want to argue that Freud's strange short paper from 1935, 'The Subtleties of a Faulty Action', is a reading of the death drive, a performance of it, including its stakes for psychoanalysis itself. The lesson on face value seems rather commonplace – namely the analysability of lapses, something Freud certainly already established. Two pages at most in length, it was written just before the much more famous 'A Disturbance of Memory on the Acropolis' (1936). Freud moves from faulty symptomatic action to disturbances of memory and time; one seems to focus on women and daughters, the other on fathers and brothers. In the 'Faulty Action' paper, the mistake that takes centre stage is a slip of the pen, a mistake when writing out instructions for a gift, the smallest of mistakes that conceals a 'large number of premises and dynamic determinants'.[1] Small mistakes, large motives.

It is as if Freud needed to remind us that faulty action is not necessarily obvious or robust, but subtle. Hiding in plain sight usually invokes the presence of death in Freud. And in this self-study, the question of subtlety is a reminder to the analyst that all self-analysis is incomplete, that our judgements of value follow our wish for happiness, that our actions often fail or symptomatically short-circuit, and, finally, that none of us can look death squarely in the face. Maybe the subtlety of a faulty action will call us to order, remind us that analysis is interminable. And perhaps this repetition, this persistence, is something we can endure, less as a burden or fault, but more simply as the condition of living, especially living with others.

It would probably do us good to remember that a fault is not only a mistake but also an opening, a crevice into which one might fall. Freud insinuates that his mistake isn't a mistake, it is the attempt at a mistake, a word that is written and crossed out immediately, a mistake that autocorrected another mistake, a stylistic repetition that the mistaken word alerted Freud to. This is the subtlety. But it is precisely here that this paper folds in on itself.

On a card accompanying a gift Freud accidently writes the word *bis* – which means 'until' in German and 'for a second time' in Latin – at a point in which he also wrote *für* – 'for' – twice, 'in rapid succession'. This repetition of *für* 'sounded ugly and should be avoided'.[2] The phonetic equivocal meaning in two languages of *bis* – 'until' and 'for a second time' – links with the German *für* and substitutes for it. Freud is alerted to the repetition of *für* by the internal repetition inherent to *bis*, which he remembers in the Latin expression *Ne bis in idem*, 'Do not institute the same proceedings twice', a maxim of Roman law. Or *Bis! Bis!* in French, when Frenchmen cry for a repeat performance, an encore. The action thus stretches between giving, for, until, for a second time, again, never again, not twice, and the paradoxical maxim 'do not institute the same proceedings twice'.

The immediacy of action in the giving of a gift is interrupted by a slight mistake which introduces a delay, an interval – 'until' – allowing a question: *More, or never again?* The mistake achieves significance not in being made, but in being corrected. The repetition is done away with, or undone, though the undoing itself points to the sheer 'institution' of repetition. This structure is explicit, Freud says, in many blunders. The faulty action then is not an action at all, but an undoing of action, an action that points to its own undoing, and this doing and undoing as the force of repetition.

What is fascinating is that Freud says he would have been satisfied with this aesthetic explanation, the removal of the rather ugly repetition of *für*, except that one needs avoid the danger of incomplete interpretation when it comes to self-analysis. We should not be satisfied too quickly. There is more. *Bis!* Freud turns the example over to his daughter, Anna Freud, who reminded him that he had given the same gift to the same woman already. The woman happened to be Dorothy Burlingham, the American child psychoanalyst, and this repeated gift to her was most likely the repetition he wanted to avoid.

Behind the repetition of the word, and the wrong word for seemingly the right action, we find yet another repetition – this time in reality – of the gift: the same ring with an engraved gem. Why does Freud want to give this gift twice? In fact, it seems that he didn't *not* want to give the gift again as an act of impropriety, but rather that, in the first place, he never wanted to give it at all. 'For it is easy to discover the further sequel. I was looking for a motive for not making a present of the stone, and that motive was provided by the reflection that I had already made the same (or a very similar) present. Why should this object have been concealed or disguised? Very soon I saw clearly why. I wanted not to give the stone away at all. I liked it very much myself.'[3]

In giving the gift twice, he would have created a motive not to give the gift to Dorothy Burlingham but to himself. Freud consoles himself with the thought that 'regrets of this kind only enhance the value of the gift. What sort of gift would it be if one were not a little bit sorry to part with it?'[4] This repetition raises the gift to a second power: Freud is not just giving it twice but potentially losing it twice. It functions as both this double loss, while also being yet another renunciation of the act of giving, a reassertion of selfishness.

To really give something, Freud says, one must experience the gift as a loss – which isn't a given – and it is this potential experience of loss which makes its appearance in the paper in the repetition, in the space between *again and again* and *never again*. An intense ambivalence appears, and it isn't clear whether the never again – the figure of death – is what he is trying to prevent, or encounter. Losing it twice: it is an action that is not simply an undoing of a prior action but an action intensified through repetition. Even further, he brings in his daughter – implicated in the gift – to supposedly check that his analysis is sound, moving closer to action, to repetition in reality.

Why did Freud write this short text in 1935? Perhaps we ought to link this paper to his next, 'A Disturbance of Memory on the Acropolis' from 1936, where there is an affective play between having gone too far, the experience of unreality, and filial piety. Freud, visiting the Acropolis with his brother, interprets his disbelief as a disturbance of memory, a tear in the fabric of reality that happens on the basis of confronting a moment of surpassing his own father, who was too poor to travel. *So it exists!* is a translation of *I never thought I would make it this far*, or, *This is too good to be true*. Freud is talking about the unreality that comes from crossing a certain line, from fulfilling a long-held wish, sliding between a half-gift and the deathly fulfilment of a desire.[5]

Guilt appears in this doubling of consciousness – this is and is not happening – which evokes a certain low mood. Even further, disavowed satisfaction, says Freud, can serve as a strong motive to fall ill, which is opposed to the general rule of neurotic illness as a result of frustration. This reversal in the symptom Freud calls the intergenerational transmission of guilt through the super-ego – the death drive passed down – seen best in how it haunts those who are wrecked by success, who can receive nothing. The limit is set, the threat is marked. One is commanded: *Do not go further than where I am. Do not satisfy yourself!* The subject is warned that beyond this point unbinding will take place.

'Analysis Terminable and Interminable', written by Freud in 1937, is foreshadowed in the 1935 paper on 'The Subtleties of a Faulty Action'. The 'Faulty Action' paper can be read as a warning to future analysts against incomplete analysis. If Freud claims that there is a bedrock refusal of castration or death, that the death drive is unrelenting, is analysis unending? If an obstinate desire for mastery is equally present in both sexes, where illness is preferable to cure, then is analysis unending? Freud says the most difficult point is when the patient must recognise the help coming from the other. It is here that most analyses break down. The question of what can be exchanged is also here a question for Freud about the institution of psychoanalysis itself.

The problem that Freud is outlining in 1937 concerns the 'negative therapeutic reaction', or the negative side of transference – hate, not love, or ambivalence more generally. The patient wants to remain ill, to show his hate rather than get well as a result of his love. This conundrum was first signalled in the 1920s when the early success of psychoanalytic treatments seemed to disappear. The insights had grown too commonplace, or insight, in the way it was conceived at that time, wasn't proving any longer to be the operative force of treatment, causing Freud to rewrite the economics of the libido. Freud situates a beyond where the difference between what is pleasure and what is unpleasure, what is life and what is death, what is love and what is hate, what is a gift and what isn't, is much more difficult to distinguish or hold, all of which seems to invite the compulsion to repeat, which is not simply the repetition of some pleasure or even unpleasure, but a repetition looking to mark some extreme limit or threshold.

The relentlessness of this beyond, the difficulty of this marking, is why analysts may need to return, again and again, for analysis, like maintenance or a hygienic practice. Even Freud, who was never analysed, said this. The beyond of the pleasure principle itself is the problem of the more and more, the again and again necessary at this frontier. For Lacan, the analyst must be possessed by this more, this monstrousness of the drive in the form of the desire of the analyst, something that he also calls 'the ethics of psychoanalysis'.[6] A strange reversal, but that's Lacan for you.

If, for Freud, love was always an illusion that would eventually betray one's ambivalence and death wish towards loved ones, Lacan was someone for whom death could become the gift of love, the giving and receiving of nothing, something we can write again and again. For Lacan, love is this writing. Is this not also the very paradoxical definition of what a psychoanalytic institution must be as group of people centred on a love of the unconscious? And isn't this what psychoanalysis guarantees – a frame in order to address this unending work?

Lacan's definition of love thus tries to account for Freud's beyond by giving room to the ever-present fault and faulty actions of loving partners. He says that it was precisely this double movement in Freud that affected him deeply. It is where he began with psychoanalysis:

> The beginning of wisdom should involve beginning to realize that it is in that respect [on the question of love] that old father Freud broke new ground. I myself began with that because it affected me quite a bit. It could affect anyone, moreover, couldn't it, to realize that love, while it is true that it has a relationship with the One, never makes anyone leave himself behind . . . How can there be love for another?[7]

In this Lacanian vein, Freud's love tokens, the death rings, may signify the recognition of frailty and fault, rather than its refusal. The ring is not a symbol of the One, the unity of Freud and his followers in a parodic church, but the gift of an enclosed hole, the hole that is transferred from analyst to analyst, from one to another one. Perhaps Freud repeated the foundational truth of faulty action at the end of his life, handing over his half-analysis to his daughter as an *I do not know what I am doing* that could have been taken up by her, by all of us. *But I never wanted to give anyone anything in the first place*, Freud comically insists. Or perhaps better, my gift was a gift of nothing. Freud's desire is not only in question, it is put into question again and again, as an interminable encore.

Loneliness

I don't think I've ever felt as lonely as I have in analytic training, but a characteristic of loneliness is its egocentric magnitude accompanied by amnesia for any other time of having been lonely, as if loneliness lifts by virtue of repression only to descend again with implacable immediacy. There is a singular quality to the loneliness of being a candidate in analytic training. Perhaps a movement from loneliness to solitude can be found; one critical to the act of learning to listen, learning to use one's unconscious life, to take bearing there. Perhaps even a question of how analytic training might support or hinder the transformation of loneliness could be wrestled with, tentatively.

On first glance, the intensity of loneliness that I experienced as a candidate seems ripe for an interpretation of repetition. How did you experience being in school? Disappointment more generally? What were your expectations? Where did those expectations come from? Were you a lonely child? What did analytic training wake up in you from your past? Behind all this is a more structural question. What does it mean to be a candidate? What can we say about the experience of being a candidate, of being in the middle of that strange, difficult and absolutely unique experience of taking up the position of the analyst for the first time? It is a knife's edge between the personal history that one brings to psychoanalytic training and the history of psychoanalysis itself, its formation of a training system.

I remember an email that went around my institute, written by a fellow candidate who spoke with enthusiasm about how proud she was to be part of this historic place and its many masterful clinicians, evoking a potent image of family and lineage. A lingering despair about training and institutes always hit hard at moments like this, along with a certain amount of guilty rage, self-accusation, and intense loneliness. Why didn't I feel this way? Where was my gratitude? Thinking about the loneliness of the candidate, my own mythic story kept surfacing in my mind, one that has acted like a life raft throughout training. I return to it again and again. I realised, while reflecting upon it, that it was a story of the anti-candidate, a story of a non-training training, if only because there was really nowhere to train, no institute, and only the slightest idea of what psychoanalysis should make possible. In imagination, absent these structures, the desire for psychoanalysis seems to have had an inordinate amount of room to take shape. This is what gives it its mythic character.

The story is about the utmost point of solitude present when taking on a case, taking responsibility as a psychoanalyst, which can be seen so clearly because there are almost no extant supports. We need extremes not to establish a middle road but to clarify what is universal. This is what I find so extraordinary about Freud's methodology, taking perversion and establishing the place of psychosexual development in all human beings, taking dreams and situating the unconscious, taking psychosis even and delineating the power of desire in both defence and cure.

A woman named Rosine Lefort, thirty years old, begins her analysis with Lacan in Paris in the early 1950s. A year and a half later she starts work in a hospital, the Parent de Rosan Foundation, under the direction of the paediatrician and soon-to-be psychoanalyst Jenny Aubry (mother of Élisabeth Roudinesco, the great historian of French psychoanalysis and herself a psychoanalyst). Rosine was to work with children between the ages of one and four who had either been abandoned by their families or who were being cared for in the hospital because of the illness of their sole living parent. The hospital did not understand the difference between physical and mental illness, and these children were left in bed for most of the day. Rosine describes the children watching a nurse feed them one by one, each knowing full well their place in this line. Crying, watching, waiting; three times a day, this is how meals were taken.

Paris was a little behind the times with respect to psychoanalysis because of the Second World War and a general resistance to psychoanalysis that didn't exist as strongly in the Germanophone and Anglo-American worlds. In anticipation of the Occupation, the Société Psychanalytique de Paris had been entirely dissolved. But, it must be said, even in its minimal existence before the war, it had had very little impact on the hospital systems which were dominated by a long and very orthodox tradition of French psychiatry going back to Jean-Martin Charcot and Pierre Janet, and including figures like Gaëtan de Clérambault and Henri Claude. The hospitals were seen as places for expanding the knowledge and research of French psychiatry and its classification systems rather than as treatment centres. Psychoanalysis was a huge source of contention in this regard.

Jenny Aubry was working with Françoise Dolto, one of the first child psychoanalysts in France. Both Aubry and Dolto were consulting with Anna Freud, Melanie Klein, D.W. Winnicott and the Tavistock more generally. They were interested in the work of René Spitz and John Bowlby, the latter directing an international study on hospitalised children that partially funded Aubry's work and which must have served in the financial support for Rosine's position at the hospital. They were also working with Lacan.

Aubry was writing an important book entitled *Enfance abandonnée* looking at the exacerbation or creation of illness in these children by virtue of their prolonged hospitalisation. She was hoping, obviously, to change the way the mentally ill were treated in France. Rosine Lefort, beginning her work, takes four children into psychoanalysis who seem on the verge of psychosis. The work with her first two cases, the thirteen-month-old Nadia in particular, is incredibly intense. Work with Nadia – which one can read about in the most extraordinary and unprecedented detail – seems to demand that Rosine use all of herself to help this child, whose health was alarmingly in decline in the manner of a 'failure to thrive'. Something in Nadia's eyes, the pleasure she takes in looking and playing at exchanging gazes despite an almost total passivity, draws Rosine to work with her first. There was some contact that Nadia still wanted to make; there were signs of life. Rosine takes Nadia down to a playroom for sessions five times a week.

In the beginning months of treatment Rosine interprets that Nadia is attempting to extract an object from her body that she can tolerate as separate. If it is acknowledged as separate it could be a source of desire. For Rosine, this is an encounter with a point of loss that is nearly unbearable for her, this case giving us something of the fierce link between being able to desire and having to inevitably confront loss in doing so. We want what we do not have: desire shows us our dependency on outside forces.

Alone in our desires, we must reach outwards towards the world, a fact that Rosine sees as literally giving us an inside and outside, marking the difference, the crucial gap between the two. For her, desire gives birth to us as human beings, creatures formed in a knotting of drive, desire and loss. Childhood psychosis, psychosis in general, refuses to allow this knot to form, taking instead the route of a kind of dispersal of these threads in drive diffusion, dedifferentiation, and autistic-like encapsulation. Desire, as a subject-forming force, is foreclosed.

The scene that comes to mind is when Nadia, finally building up the courage to have more contact with Rosine, seeks out her mouth, tracing it, and putting her fingers into it, and then touching her own. She bites off the corner of a cracker and then has Rosine do the same. Confronted with this minimal differentiation between her mouth and Rosine's

– finding her own mouth by taking in the image of another's – she becomes incredibly violent, clawing and scratching at Rosine's neck. Rosine interprets this as both as a defence against having registered the place of her mouth (there is no hole in one's neck) and a primordial symbolisation of what she just encountered.[1]

It is important to see this act of symbolisation even in negation and violent acting-out. It was a decisive step in the treatment, a possibility opened up in the transference where objects could enter into an economy of exchange, as Rosine sees it, in the form of oral, anal and phallic signifiers. Nadia had to refuse, but in this first act of refusal she recognises a gap between herself and what she wants. In this wanting, she begins to structure her self-image. The mouth was her first critical object, important since Nadia was barely eating, didn't use her mouth to suck, and seemed to take little to no oral pleasure, which was a situation so severe that her health was in rapid decline.[2]

In sessions Nadia had pulled at Rosine's fingers, her teeth and skin, but the mouth increasingly became the centre of her attention, proving to be hollow, a ready-made gap for an investigation of what cannot be filled. Having been filled passively by nurses for the majority of her life, treated as an inert body, one begins to see what is at stake. Rosine conjectures that in the pull towards psychosis, there is no mouth, no orifice that acts as a site of exchange. There is no hole in the body, which, taken in this psychotic totality, acts like a smooth surface with nothing lacking. Psychosis is a denial of separation whose smooth surface anchors nothing, no self-image, no other.[3]

Rosine has to work against this regressive pull, to open a space for desire and wish. But aggressivity immediately erupts in Nadia when desire is felt. Rosine writes of this experience,

> I was only too sensitive to the limits she imposed on
> me, having myself suffered from neurosis. It had been

through my body that I had experienced this suffering intensely; a body which, as always in such cases, I could only cope with by allowing it to become the object of care and attention. Nadia, for her part, only had her body in so far as it was the object of care and attention. The ambiguous solicitations of care givers, whether in the family or in an institution, can leave the subject in the totally derelict state of being physically manipulated in the Real, without a single word to acknowledge her position as subject. As a result of this painful experience, I was reluctant to become a maternal figure for her, that is to say, to give additional care and attention and, inconsiderately, to bring into play the Real of bodies, of the child's and mine . . . In the analytic relationship that established itself, Nadia put me in a position where she showed me the Real character of my body, while at the same time forcing me to renounce it. It was in this position that I was to let her challenge me, to listen to what she had to say, to let her speak death in order to live.[4]

Rosine works for a little over a year trying to reverse the consequences of Nadia's illness and we can see that in it she is already making reference to her own 'neurosis', to something she knows about how a body feels in neurotic suffering. Through this, she is able to recognise the first rumblings of desire – death – in the unfolding of their relationship in the transference.

Nadia must emerge as a subject in her own right, but her illness is such that despite the fact that this is exactly what she needs, it is exactly what she refuses. Rosine understands how this child neurotically solicits (already at the age of thirteen months) exactly the inapposite care to what is required in this task of becoming a subject. Rosine cannot confuse this register of acknowledgement with mothering this little girl, reducing listening to an exchange of caresses that would silence her. Doing so would mean a certain kind of renunciation. These are renunciations we all have to learn to make when taking up the position of the analyst, but here we see specifically how it takes place on the level of the body. Yes, this is a pre-verbal child, but Nadia, I think, shows us the original principle of abstinence, the necessity that a demand for bodily exchange be exchanged, at all costs, for words born of desire. It is only in them that we may hope to find ourselves. Nadia brings Rosine to this basic psychoanalytic truth.

One could imagine that *only* psychoanalysis – ensconced in the mythic proportions I lent to it while a candidate – could make this possible. Only psychoanalysis could bring a child back in this way, refusing to confuse care in the form of mental hygiene with what must more enduringly take place. And it is not simply 'better care' than that of the nurses. It is not the well-ordered ministrations of a doctor. Psychoanalysis cannot participate in this form of morality. The question of what gives birth to a subject, separate from a body, separate from simply biological life, is the guiding question for Rosine.

This is what is so astonishing in this work: as you read you read her traversing this edge between a care that makes passive and silences and this other thing called psychoanalysis. You watch Rosine invent psychoanalysis by figuring out how to differentiate the two. It isn't obvious, and what you also learn is that it wouldn't be so even for the 'fully' trained psychoanalyst – a reassuring fact for a candidate no doubt. That Rosine is able to do so is what saves Nadia. Inventing herself as a psychoanalyst becomes synonymous with this child's cure. Their fates are completely intertwined.

It is here for me, in this moment, that the stage is set for the mythic action. This is the point where what Rosine is in the process of inventing will be shown to enter into her life more broadly. Forming herself as a psychoanalyst becomes an operating force whose lines read like the lines of fate. Isn't that always how a myth unfolds? An action is taken that will come to shape a life with the force of destiny, already foretold by an oracle of some kind, like a message from Cassandra that no one can hear. Doesn't fate always unfold from a moment of critical choice, Rosine standing at the crossroads?

This choice point brings itself to bear on her very life: the intensity of Rosine's work with Nadia (and soon to include three others) is so great, calls on her to use her own experience of illness to such an extent, that she feels she cannot continue with her personal analysis at the same time. The choice feels like an either/or, either her analysis or theirs. The two cannot co-exist. Rosine decides she has to leave her analysis until she feels like she can handle both again. She chooses Nadia over herself and, perhaps, over Lacan. The hiatus lasts for thirteen months, the time that she is working in the hospital with these four children.[5]

This is the moment I return to again and again in my imagination. I've thought about the choice Rosine felt she had to make, the position she put her analyst in. Did Lacan interpret this decision as a defence, as a part of the transference neurosis? Did he make her feel that the antithetical choice was part of her illness or a counter-transference that must be analysed? Did he support her desire to leave and its connection to what was so painful about keeping herself and these children in mind simultaneously? Was the work itself seen as a reasonable substitute for a period of time to establish her analytic identity? Did he affirm her position as psychoanalyst, where desire is precisely a force that calls on you to make a decision, one that hangs in the balance like life and death? What did Lacan do? While I have it all mapped out, just as I'm describing it now, the strange irony is that very little is actually written about this moment by Rosine herself.

Looking at her work I was surprised by how sparse the indication of this moment is, compared not only to my imagination of it, but to what it is in distinction to the immense work on the cases themselves (Nadia's alone over two hundred pages). Rosine writes,

Nadia's treatment was the first chronologically. It will be
shown how I started it. This treatment lasted approxi-
mately ten months, from October 1951 until July 1952.
By October 1951 I had been in analysis for eighteen
months. My analysis had been imposed by the need to
overcome neurotic suffering and for that reason it was
very difficult for me. It was difficult to the point that
during Nadia's treatment I felt, over a period of several
months, that it was impossible for me to attend the sessions of my own analysis regularly. The treatment of
Nadia, and indeed of the other children which I com-
menced successively in the course of the following
three months, in some way performed the function,
therefore, of a substitute in my own analytic process,
within which it came to be inscribed.[6]

With that she ends her preface. I realised that it wasn't what
she said about her analysis, or her own suffering per se, but
what one reads *from* this, between the lines of the case, that
finally gives you an indication of the profound passage she is
making. She gives you the hint and you follow the scent in the
unfolding story of her work with Nadia.

If one thinks of myths – and clearly I am working with
their classical form – life-changing passages are traversed by
virtue of forced exile, confronting the necessity of sacrifice,
a dangerous odyssey, or simply the unknown. This change
of order always involves a radical separation from ancestors,
family and home. The passage indelibly inscribes something
in its *passant*. My thoughts turn here because the final word
that Rosine uses in her preface is 'inscribed'. Something
needed to be inscribed – a word whose dual meaning is 'to
carve, write or mark, in an enduring way', and 'to name, ded-
icate or sign', from the Latin *inscribere*.

We know that Freud spoke of the unconscious as a kind
of writing, as a magical writing tablet whose traces form a
matrix of wish and memory. But these memory traces in the

unconscious are also organised around traumatic moments, in particular, inevitable experiences of loss in the context of one's developing (sexual) self. Trauma means wound, puncture, opening, and is tied to the body. We erase some of the original meaning of the unconscious as traumatic writing in a contemporary ideology that positions trauma as simply bad, as compared to those who are supposedly 'not' traumatised. For Freud, sexuality is inevitably traumatic even in the very force that drive exerts upon mind. Wrestling with these forces can bring about something new in subjectivity.

Attempting to return to this original meaning, I would say that Rosine's act of leaving her analysis does just this. It punctuates or marks by creating a gap, and this gap provides a space, an opening, for her desire as a psychoanalyst. It was no doubt traumatic in the sense just described, something that was exerting force from the inside, and Rosine had to find whatever way possible to sustain this tension, to live through it. Her pioneering work with children, through this absence, is inscribed into her analysis, and her analysis circumscribes this moment, absent though she was, when she takes up the position of the analyst.

The image is like that of a circle with a hole, a figure like that of the mouth, or any orifice whose rim-like structure psychoanalysis has shown as the erogenous sites of sexuality. The rim is a threshold between inside and outside. Allowing the drive to circumscribe this threshold, to symbolise and signify a point of interchange, the body becomes a written body, a body with a potential for language, creativity, sublimation. It is, as Rosine poetically puts it, the writing of a hole, like what it means to see with one's mouth, as Spitz once characterised the baby.[7]

Try though we may, all erogenous zones starting with the mouth are hollows that ultimately cannot be filled. Trying – why call this desire anyway – forms a subject with an inside and an outside. Lacan spoke of this formation once, as a glove turning inside out, a Möbius strip's inside surface that traverses simultaneous to its outside edge.[8] The most basic self-image is formed thus and it is a radical act of naming, of being called into being. Freud wrote that the ego is first and foremost a body ego, and Rosine means to find these earliest moments when the body first becomes a written body, binding drive in the nascent structure of the ego. Lacan, of course, elaborates these concepts theoretically in his paper on the mirror stage.

Rosine writes about a slip in her notes where she forgot to mention Nadia wanting her to help her look in the mirror before the end of the session:

> I can say that Nadia's treatment, in the full sense of the word, was a part of my own analysis, since it was with and through her that I was to come to grips with my own specular image, or rather with its relations with the Other. It was an exemplary illustration of, on the one hand, the place of the analyst as the one who is taught by the analysand; but much more than teaching, it was a question of the essential unconscious passage that this baby-analysand was to cause me to make. After treating Nadia, standing in front of a mirror was quite a different experience for me.[9]

A dual inscription indeed. If the analysand is not the one to teach the analyst, then how can this dual inscription take place? This kind of unconscious writing – what she calls an unconscious passage – is how Rosine Lefort will come to define analytic work. The self-image of analyst and analysand are mutually altered.

Once you have the action that crystallises a myth it is important to understand its aftermath, the trajectory of what it has set in motion through this inscription, like everything that follows in the wake of Antigone's decision to bury her brother, Polynices, in defiance of Creon's laws. Lacan encouraged Rosine to present some of her work four years later in

his newly formed seminar that would serve as the foundation
of the École Freudienne de Paris. These cases were seen as
an important and inaugural application of French psychoanalytic ideas to work with severely ill children. Jenny Aubry,
Françoise Dolto and Rosine Lefort continued to expand child
psychoanalysis in France in the 60s and 70s.

Rosine joins Maud Mannoni, another heroic figure in
my mind, in her experiments with in-patient settings and the
treatment of severe illness from pseudo-mental retardation
to schizophrenia and autism at the École Expérimentale in
Bonneuil-sur-Marne in the southeastern suburbs of Paris.
Mannoni wrote extensively on working with families and
within institutions, developing a place for psychoanalysts in
the most divergent of settings, showing how psychoanalysis is
uniquely situated for the most crucial interventions in these
settings. Figures like Gilles Deleuze, Félix Guattari and others came to Bonneuil – which became legendary – to work
and develop their ideas on psychoanalysis and its relation to
a whole host of disciplines including theatre, politics, art and
philosophy, creating a public intellectual space for the discussion of psychoanalysis. Rosine Lefort publishes these cases as
a book, but only thirty years later. Seeing this arc, you know
that she never could have calculated its endpoint.

I would reiterate that I do not and would not make a
judgement on Rosine's need to leave analysis – she certainly doesn't. In fact, precisely the opposite, since what
she uniquely transmits in this text is the powerful desire
of a psychoanalyst that she alluded to having been born in
that decision. One could even say she demonstrates this as a
desire that lasts a lifetime. Transmitting this desire through
a written text is a difficult task and is, in my opinion, rarely
communicated; this desire is easily blotted out by one's theoretical allegiance, institutional commitments, or simply the
heavy weight of fetishised knowledge. If you want to convey
desire, there is very little room for the super-egoic, whose
shape-shifting prose properties within a discipline should be

examined. Rosine, to my mind, manages.

Something new must be created at all costs and the unconscious passage necessary for this creation is harrowing and often very, very lonely. The difficulty of sustaining the analytic position in the face of the youngest of patients in an extreme situation is what I find so path-breaking in Rosine's work. And this, in particular, by an analyst who could have no guarantee of her position, of her work, or even of her status, being without formal training, having abandoned her own analysis, shy of most conceptual developments in France with respect to theory and technique.

The pull of a pernicious rescue fantasy could only have been incredibly intense and yet, as she would have known, this would have been a total violation of the analytic frame. I can only imagine the pull between this fantasy and her identification with the principles of a psychoanalytic process, one that she had only begun to experience herself eighteen months previously. How did she do this? She develops a laser-like focus, finding any way to allow the objects – whether it is food or toys or parts of her own body – to take on a symbolic dimension in the transference. It is the most intimate and minute of confrontations with these objects treated only as signifiers in the transference that seemingly brings the child out of her impasse.

What this means is that these objects are not taken as objects to fill a lack, to stuff a body, but heard as signifiers that Rosine marks not only through interpretation but by attention, for example, to her presence in distinction to that of the nurses on the ward. She creates the treatment and its frame. The frame isn't there already, as if by calling yourself an analyst it just exists. The frame is something you create through listening as a psychoanalyst with only the conviction of what it must make possible.

Psychoanalysis is an act of creativity, one taken on in absolute solitude, especially in the beginning. The easiest way to deal with this loneliness – the self-reliance and sense of

one's own illness that is called on – is by thwarting the analytic process and replacing it with something that *feels* more
substantial. A fantasy of rescue, and the call to the child would
be to speak to me, for me, not for his or her self.

If loneliness runs like a flat line, an insomniac night,
all-pervasive and unending, then there is something important here about what disrupts a state of things, what breaks
into loneliness and transforms it, what makes loneliness a
force of creativity. I would say it has something to do with
desire's sublimation form. Desire's negative underside is
loneliness. One is inevitably lonely in one's desire. To desire
is to accept loneliness in the form of solitude, which finally
gives birth to new possibilities.

Rosine uses her analysis, *even when leaving it*, in order to
sustain her transferential work with these children. Doing so
creates her as a psychoanalyst and creates a link to the field as
a whole. This is how French psychoanalysis would eventually
come to understand (years after the case of Nadia) what they
call 'the desire for psychoanalysis' that binds analysts in their
impossible profession. Though we work in solitude, alone in
our offices, maintaining this social link is important. But it
is seen as nothing more than desire, founded on a profound
confrontation with loss. What this means is that it cannot be
something like a false object to fill a hole in the form of identifications with power, prestige or even family, which are a
denial of loss, loneliness and the necessity of solitude.

Finally, if desire is transformed into a desire for psychoanalysis, then it is one that we have to let trainees invent for
themselves. Becoming an analyst requires this kind of precarious invention and if training lapses into indoctrination in
any form, into a prescribed way of doing things, it thwarts this
process. Training would amount to a silencing of the candidate's desire. All institutional troubles follow from failing to
make this differentiation.

Psychoanalysis seems to me to have a choice: either it
can treat candidates as inert bodies to be filled (by knowledge,

with solicited identifications, varieties of quasi-maternal attention, the supposedly rescuing structure of an authority), mistaking this kind of care for helping candidates find their way as analysts, or it can work to create or open a space in which it hopes, but cannot know, that a desire for psychoanalysis will be born.

Have we lost our ability to structure analytic training in accordance with what we know about the engendering of desire? When one cannot locate a space for desire in one's training, it is created through a massive split. The next generation finds a voice, but questions of an enduring transmission of psychoanalysis between generations are left in the wings, the field fragmenting generation after generation. Are we caught in the infinite creation of psychoanalytic institutes? It is important to hear in our theory that our process is a process of mobilising this thing we call psychoanalysis in a way that speaks more broadly to what it means to be a psychoanalyst. It helps bind the generations in a structure of inherited desire.

Rosine Lefort could not have allowed herself to feel pity for these children she was working with if she was to keep to the frame of what psychoanalysis was to try and open. She had to rely on her desire. The analyst has to place him or herself beyond loneliness in a realm where solitude can take on the strength of a desire that is beyond fear and beyond pity. Loneliness, even exclusion, is fundamental to Klein and Lacan, and their way of conceiving subjectivity. Of course, for both of these thinkers, as well as for Rosine, as we have seen, this work is tied to the act of symbolisation. Symbolisation is for them not a vague, easy or once-and-for-all matter. For Lacan the symbolisation of desire means you confront the most fundamental of losses, as well as find the courage to face the super-egoic social pressures that like to keep symbolisation and pleasure in check. For Klein it means you are able to get one foot out the door of unavoidable paranoid splitting while still facing the harangue of depressive anxieties. A harsh super-ego will never forgive destructive impulses, and the harsher the super-ego the greater will be one's loneliness and need for defence. This amounts, for Klein, to an imperative to find a way to allow enjoyment to mitigate destructive impulses even when that is at the cost of the hopelessness and disappointment of de-idealisation.[10]

The kind of creativity and capacity for pleasure that psychoanalysis must constantly reinvent in order to move forward is an idea that I feel has supported me in the darkest moments of training.

Rosine's transference transfers to psychoanalysis itself, to its internal principles in their most basic form – co-ordinates that could serve as the beginning of an entire life. It is for this reason that I imagine she can practise as a psychoanalyst in the most divergent of settings. She ends her case with Nadia in this fashion:

> On May 20th she gave me the most poetic image of herself: through the window, I saw her in the garden, playing with her shadow, clapping with joy at the way it changed shape. Death was there, although she did not know it; it was life she was applauding . . . This is the point Nadia had reached . . . the transference was not the enactment of the unconscious but the place where the unconscious could emerge, the place where Nadia as subject could emerge . . . Hence she was able to detach herself from me . . . At the time I said, 'we have nothing more to do together'.[11]

There Is No Common Satisfaction

In early Freud anxiety is linked to the failure of the sexual. Orgasm, he tells us, is the ejection into the outside of the scraps or grains of libido, the exteriorisation of the drive in bodily coitus. Anxiety is these scraps trapped on the inside, unable to enter the stream of thought, or to simply return to the body, caught between here and nowhere. The failure of the sexual makes us anxious, because it reminds us that there is no common satisfaction; there is only this singular process of externalising sexual libido.[1]

Lacan, speaking about this failure of the sexual, uses a surreal naturalistic fable of a shrimp that needs to imbibe a grain of sand to establish its equilibrium. The grain is discarded and replaced in each moulting cycle; without the pull of gravity from this grain the shrimp would be constantly disorientated in the tides. The shrimp, Lacan says, first needs to take this outside inside. But it has to be the right grain of sand. The shrimp has to find this right grain of sand at all costs – scientists forced them swallow all kinds of things that set them off balance, including fragments of metal that allowed the scientists to play with these poor shrimps using magnets.[2] Strange that evolution can make room for something like this.

Some early psychoanalysts tried to explain anxiety by the idea of the shock of birth, the separation from the mother's body. Freud didn't buy this; if this was so, then everyone would be crippled by virtue of being born. Lacan says, let us think of the shrimp: a foreign exterior, not so unlike oxygen, breath, must invade us from the outside. Being born, breathing, imbibing, expelling, exhaling, losing, form the continuum of life as sex life.

What do we do about anxiety? 1) *There is no common satisfaction.* Don't let it deter you. 2) *Stop feeling scared of losing things.* What control did you ever have in the first place? 3) *Imbibe sand like a shrimp and find your equilibrium.* Find your grain of sand, take it in from the other, give it away, start over.

Masturbation Fantasies

There's a psychoanalytic myth that until you've fully unearthed, deconstructed and analysed a patient's masturbation fantasy their treatment is incomplete. In fact, the idea is that this fantasy runs so deep that it structures their entire life – the partners or jobs they choose, how they fail or succeed in love and work, and certainly what gives them pleasure and what turns them off. It is almost as if this masturbatory scene were a film silently running in the background of life, determining the playbook, grafting itself onto the future, condensing an entire sexual and familial history into a thirty-second, three-line script. What else could explain the ubiquity and specificity of pornography? How else to understand the tendencies toward fixation and repetition in our romantic lives?

'A Child Is Being Beaten' is Freud's paper on the topic of masturbation fantasies. Published in 1919, we now know that the paper was written about his daughter Anna Freud, whose masturbatory beating fantasies he tried to disguise as a discussion about a case. But they could only have come from her – as told to her father Freud, who analysed her – because at the time he wrote the paper he hadn't started seeing patients yet. These are the secret incestuous boundary-violating origins of the Freudian quest for masturbation fantasies to interrogate.

Freud wrote this paper in order to correct what he was beginning to suspect was a trend in psychoanalysis by which these fantasies were being thought of as a perversion – a kind of developmental failure to make it to some sort of sexual normality. Freud says instead that they are common and that they are like a kind of scar or afterbirth, a residue, of what inevitably fails in our attempt to become adult sexual human beings. In fact, these fantasies show us the main components of our sexual lives, like a prism absorbing white light to then reveal to us all the gradations of colour that compose it.[1]

The conscious masturbatory fantasy is reported by patients, Freud says, only with extreme difficulty. This was especially the case with several women who could only report their fantasy through the ambiguous and strange sentence, 'A child is being beaten'. Freud wonders if this scene is tied to a traumatic memory, perhaps of having been spanked. There are also childhood memories of seeing other kids being punished, but these don't appear particularly remarkable.[2] More important, Freud decides, is the scene as an index of rivalry between children and the bid for love and recognition from the parental, authority figure; or as Freud puts it: *He beats him, he loves me.* This beating also represents the action of masturbation itself – to beat off.[3]

Freud says that the most unconscious layer of the fantasy, one that he says is never actually remembered and that must be constructed by the analyst, is this: 'I am being beaten by my father.' So, in the masturbation fantasy, at least as Freud describes it over one hundred years ago, there are three layers: 1) memory: *My father is beating a child (whom I hate – he loves only me)*; 2) unconscious fantasy: *I am being beaten by my father*; and 3) conscious masturbatory fantasy: *A child is being beaten* (which is revealed as: *Many children (often boys) are being beaten by a representative from the class of fathers, using a variety of instruments*).[4]

It is interesting that the analyst, in constructing the second layer for the patient, returns a more active 'I' to them, for in the other scenes the person is usually a voyeur, watching things from the sidelines. Importantly, in the conscious layer of the masturbation fantasy, which often takes place as a kind of daydream or mind-movie, what we see is that many changes are made, and elements are elaborated, which are quite revealing. For instance:

— The sex of the fantasising woman is changed to a little boy or the ambiguous 'children', pointing to some kind of erasure of the feminine.

— More than this, as a presence, she is nothing but an onlooker, a gaze.

— The father is represented as anyone who is symbolic of authority, or the law.

— Sex – or what is sexually exciting – is transformed into pain, punishment, sado-masochism, and the vicissitudes of guilt often attached to these things.

We can now interpret these transformations as we would a dream. We see in the many masturbation fantasies an attempt to answer three impossible questions associated with sexuality, which comprise three things that the child cannot understand in its sexual research: 1) the vaginal orifice; 2) the inseminating role of semen; 3) what intercourse is.

These three questions point to something that will always be lacking in our knowledge, something that religion, politics, science and morality attempt to give an answer to. We can find what we have inherited from culture pertaining to the outlines of sex, deposited into our most intimate fantasies. Not only does it tell us what we think or have been told about sex, but more universally it gives us an X-ray of where we are as a society with respect to these fundamental mysteries.

Let me show you how these questions work when applied to the classic unconscious beating fantasy from Freud.

The fantasy: *I am being beaten by my father.*

The vaginal orifice: *Where is the mother and her desire?* Answer: *There is no woman in this fantasy.*

The inseminating role of semen: *What is the father, the symbol of authority and the law, in this fantasy?* Answer: *The father is a sadist in this fantasy.*

Intercourse: *What are sexual relationships, commitment, love in this fantasy?* Answer: *Sex and love are pain and punishment in this fantasy.*

As you see, one can take these three questions – the

vaginal orifice, the inseminating role of semen, and inter-course – and adapt them to analyse any fantasy. Let me now apply this matrix to a series of anonymous masturbation fantasies.

Fantasy #1

Subject: *Gay woman, thirty years old*
'I still mainly masturbate to my brain rather than to porn. Unless I'm using the Magic Wand, in which case I just blast myself and cum before I even get a chance to think about much because it happens so fast. But, yeah, when I use my hand, I come up with little movies in my head. One that I've gone to a few times involves me and my girlfriend having sex for a room full of older women, who are watching us. The room usually looks like a classic college classroom. Like an Ivy League place. The women watching us are all fully dressed. They're also kind of severe. Like they aren't touching themselves. They're more like clinical observers. And they surround us. We're in the middle of the room. In the fantasy, the sex between my girlfriend and I is usually pretty basic in terms of what we're doing – like mutual manual playing with each other. But it's also really tender, with lots of kissing and moaning. So it's like we're not fucking while these women watch us; we're making love.'

The fantasy: *I am being taught by my mother.*

The vaginal orifice: *What are women and their desire? (Which includes the desire of the mother.)* Answer: *There is no sexual woman. There are severe school ma'ams or little girls playing at being tender.*

The inseminating role of semen: *What is the father in this fantasy?* Answer: *The father is an older female college professor with a clinical gaze.*

Intercourse: *What are sexual relationships, commitment, love in this fantasy?* Answer: *Observing (and, by inference, judging and grading); not fucking, but making love, which means kissing, touching, moaning. This display of tenderness to the women who cannot understand it. Who is teaching whom?*

Fantasy #2

Subject: *Straight man, thirty-four years old*
'I've never told anyone this before and I doubt I'll ever ask a girl to try it with me, but one of my most frequent masturbation fantasies involves farting. It's got a few specific elements though. First, I think about a girl – usually just a girl I know, like a random friend or co-worker, but never really the person I'm dating at the time – wearing black pantyhose with holes in them. She gets on her hands and knees in front of me with her butt stuck up in the air, then I find a hole in the back of her pantyhose and rip it wider so that her whole backside is exposed. Then I step away a bit and she just starts farting, basically. I usually imagine really loud, crazy farts. And I imagine her laughing while she's doing it, like it's really fun for her. Also, the farts don't smell. The scent aspect of farts is not included in the fantasy here. I don't think I'd like that part. I just focus on this image of a girl with her butt in the air surrounded by ripped black stockings, farting while she's laughing. It is sad that I'll probably never explore this fart-curious side of myself.'

The fantasy: *I am farting for my mother.*

The vaginal orifice: *What is the vagina in this fantasy?* Answer: *The vagina is an unscented farting anus in this fantasy.*

The inseminating role of semen: *What is authority in this fantasy?* Answer: *Authority is the instrument of exposing humiliation – but also the one who gives license to enjoy anal expulsion – in this fantasy.*

Intercourse: *What are sexual relationships, commitment, love in this fantasy?* Answer: *The sex is organised around 'ripping' or 'letting it rip': ripping the stocking, farting, going for it, full blast, noise. This is an almost solitary enjoyment for the one who gets to step back and watch.*

Fantasy #3

Subject: *Straight man, forty-two years old*
'I'm glad this is anonymous because I'm going to give you one that's totally baffling to me and that also feels sort of shameful, but that really gets me off whenever I think about. It starts with picturing this girl I used to go out with a long time ago. Specifically, her in her apartment when I was breaking up with her. I was being really mean, and she was crying. I feel guilty about this behaviour now, years later, and maybe that's why there's an element of shame to the fantasy. So, in real life when this happened, she was wearing nothing but a T-shirt and white cotton panties. She's wearing that in the fantasy too. The purely made-up part of it starts for me with her going into the bathroom, and me following her. I undress her and myself and I start the shower. We get in, and I spend a really long time cleaning her. I can see all the details, especially the soap bubbles on her body. I spend a lot of time cleaning her tits and her ass and her pussy. And as I'm cleaning her, she keeps crying. I picture her face with tears running down it. Just that image itself is enough to make me cum. I know this is fucked up of me, but it really gets me off.'

The fantasy: *I am being washed by my mother.*

The vaginal orifice: *What does the subject associate with women and their desire? (Which includes a question about one's mother.)* Answer: *Crying, hurt, helplessness (and, by inference, dirtiness).*

The inseminating role of semen: *What is the father in this fantasy?* Answer: *The father is the contradiction of being both the one to inflict pain and also the one washing away one's sins. Semen is soap.*

Intercourse: *What are sexual relationships, commitment, love in this fantasy?* Answer: *Anal-sadism as the transformation*

of injury into purity, or guilt into virtue. To be clean as a whistle,
to live a clean life, to have a good clean fight.

Fantasy #4

Subject: *Gay man, twenty-eight years old*
'These terms feel pretty retrograde to me, but I guess I'm
what you would call a top. I also tend to date guys who are
smaller and swishier than I am. I don't really like being with
men who have bigger muscles than me. I've never been clos-
eted (I was lucky to have cool parents and grow up in a fairly
cool town) and I have always been this way in terms of my
preferences in a partner. Also, I really don't jerk off without
the use of porn anymore. It's just faster and easier. But when
I was younger and it was still even a little bit of a struggle to
get a look at some porn, I would fantasise. One of the most
frequent fantasies I would jerk off to involved me being very
submissive and being passed around by a group of bigger
guys. Pretty much getting gangbanged. I remember thinking about struggling a little, kind of like a weak struggle, and
these fantasy guys holding me down and not letting me move
and kind of treating me like a piece of meat. Like I wouldn't
imagine them talking to me or even looking at me, but more
talking amongst themselves and joking about me or egging
each other on while they were fucking me. I've never done
anything remotely like this in my life and I doubt I ever will.
It's not like it's something I secretly want to do but I'm resist-
ing it. It's just a thing that used to come up a lot when I'd masturbate in my late teens and early twenties, and to me it feels
totally out of character.'
    The fantasy: *I am being passed around by my father.*
    The vaginal orifice: *Where is the woman in this fantasy?*
Answer: *There is no woman evident. If she is there, she is hid-*
den in the figure of the bottom, who is treated like a piece of
meat, a pure object.

The inseminating role of semen: *Where is the father in this fantasy?* Answer: *The father is a horde of men who egg each other on, talk among themselves, and help one another to hold the other down.*

Intercourse: *What are sexual relationships, commitment, love in this fantasy?* Answer: *Division between tops and bottoms, between those allowed to speak and joke and fuck but who are an indistinguishable crowd, and the one who is weak, passed around, held down, and enjoyed. Which is worse? To be the one or one of the gang?*

Fantasy #5

Subject: *Straight woman, thirty-one years old*
'This is a reversible sweater of a masturbation fantasy, and both fits are equally appealing. I get off thinking about receiving – or giving – a "sensual" massage. It goes like this: I'm lying on a table, face-down and nude. There's nothing notable about the environment; it's a pretty standard massage room. Then a man enters and begins rubbing my shoulders and my back the way massage therapists do. Sometimes I imagine the man as a person I know. Sometimes he's anonymous or even faceless. That part doesn't really matter to me too much. But it feels great. Then he starts to work my legs, my feet, and eventually my butt and inner thighs, each time stroking nearer and nearer to my vagina. Finally, he reaches it, rubs it, and fingers me until I can't hold back and beg to be fucked (and then, we do). It could also go like this: I am the one giving the massage, and the lead-up and outcome are essentially the same. I tease and touch until we fuck. The anticipation and slowly building to sex is what makes this extra-arousing to me. That aching, longing, gut-fluttering feeling. The fantasy more or less ends soon after penetration begins. It's not really about that for me. This fantasy was inspired by watching massage parlour porn; the first time I saw it I felt it was a rare

instance of a woman experiencing real sensuality in porn, instead of being ram-fucked like an animal. And I enjoy putting myself in the position of the masseuse because I totally get off on giving pleasure to my partners. In part, I think that stems from social conditioning – the importance of the male orgasm. Not that I don't believe in an equal exchange in sex.'

The fantasy: *I am being massaged by my father.*

The vaginal orifice: *What are women and their desire in this fantasy? (Which includes a question about one's mother.)* Answer: *Women are giving and receiving pleasure, begging, teasing, aching, and longing – but not being 'ram-fucked like animals'.*

The inseminating role of semen: *What is the father in this fantasy?* Answer: *The father is a sensual masseur, can take being teased, and can wait.*

Intercourse: *What are sexual relationships, commitment, love in this fantasy?* Answer: *There is a disjunction between intercourse-as-penetration and sensuality. They seem not to fit together. Penetration means the end, not the beginning. The closest one gets to a penis is a finger or the hand – hence the massage. Sensuality promises for her a more equal exchange, reversal of roles, play of tension, and ability to attend to the other's pleasure. Nevertheless, in this there is a sheer negation of the penis, and one might suspect that this is the hidden aspect of the fantasy.*

Let's consider what we've learned. These fantasies seem to point to us being just as guilty for our sexuality as we have always been – no one engages directly in the act, and the outlines of guilt, judgement, punishment and sin are everywhere. The question of fathers and authority no longer seems to be the simple figure of patriarchal law – that's withered away in the contemporary ether – but instead of the perhaps expected absence of law we find a law even more obscene and contradictory, giving paradoxical commands, or showing up in the guise of a phallic domineering woman or an unruly crowd. How true! On the side of action, fucking isn't beating but ripping, washing, teaching, passing, holding, massaging . . . Eros is a many-headed beast. Doesn't it all strike you as quite child-ish? While the search for sensuality is infinitely important, the enigma of sex and gender and love lead to a pull towards infantile sexuality such that, while there is greater symmetry between the sexes (the mother more readily appears), there is just as much debasement, if not more, and more varied. What was perhaps most striking to me was the powerful negation of the phallus in the form of a penis that cannot appear. It simply isn't there, either for the men or the women, and seems to be caught in a process of repression, or worse, negation. Is this why the phallus or phallic sexuality is reappearing in reality – questions of masculinity, toxic masculinity, rehabilitating and re-educating men? Isn't this a part of new forms of sex panic? This, while we also have a radical decline in interest in sex, 15 per cent in the US over the last few years, with the most extreme statistic coming from Japan where 47 per cent of people say they are disgusted by sexuality? Gain some, lose some: what better place to witness our Faustian bargains than in the interstices of our masturbation fantasies.

Part 4

Sex Life

Male Sexuality and Genitality

I remember a male psychoanalyst explaining how terrifying and strange erections are for young boys, a fact almost completely repressed, especially how traumatic their first ejaculatory orgasm is, the sight of this strange substance that is emitted from the penis. The feeling on the one hand is something so outside of one's control, not only desire, but also its physical manifestation, to the strange partial control that one can exert over the organ through masturbation, an act that leads to the literal disappearance of the thing – beating it, exhausting it, removing its presence, killing it metaphorically.

One of the strangest psychoanalysts, and one of my favourites, is Sándor Ferenczi, who wrote the now out-of-print book *Thalassa: A Theory of Genitality* (1933). The origins of human sexuality for the Hungarian analyst Ferenczi should be sought in the sea where we were, if not transsexual, at the very least, wholly bisexual. The goal of sea sexuality isn't penetration and reproduction within the interior of a body, it's all external, liquid, permeable, auto-sensual, and the division between the sexes in their roles in reproduction is at best murky.

Human sexuality, according to Ferenczi, is the result of geological crises throughout evolution: for example, when sea creatures were forced to live on land and breathe air, their embryos, which required a liquid environment, were more and more in jeopardy, like tadpoles clustered in a quickly evaporating puddle. Evolution, Ferenczi says, devises the strange solution of a penis that would bore into a female who would act like a host to a parasite. The sea is now inside. This is also the origin of rape, sexed reproduction requiring the domination of one half of the species.[1]

Freud also speculated on the great geological crises, saying that the first response would be, obviously, anxiety and panic, which were untenable in any prolonged fashion. The second response then would be hysteria in so far as humans would refuse all forms of sexuality and reproduction when child-rearing didn't seem optimal, making the libido a threat and causing the first psychoneurotic symptoms. The upshot, which we still see today, is that hysteria represses anxiety. The third response would be obsessional neurosis and tyranny, an act of turning away from the dangers of those suffering to the estimation of the powers of one's own thought, understanding the world not for what it is and all its attendant dangers, but according to one's ego.[2]

In a sense, Freud and Ferenczi's ideas are close: catastrophe and genitality go hand in hand, and bodily panic, or simply anxiety, is at the root of forms of domination, power, subjugation and tyranny which involve a narcissistic swerve or turning away from the world and from reality. Sexuality is either dark (thrown into suspension, repressed) or dire (the attempt to master a catastrophe in catastrophic form), or both, which is the bizarre proclamation of psychoanalytic speculation. One could appreciate the fragile lineage that brings us to today's renewed battle of the sexes in the human-dominated epoch of the Anthropocene.

Male sexuality, in so far as it has openly accommodated the avenue of tyranny most readily, is under immense scrutiny and criticism. But it isn't male sexuality as psychoanalysis thinks of it that one must address, but rather the defences to it that society – or power – harnesses towards its own unjust ends. I'm not a great believer in toxic masculinity, but rather toxic institutions, governments, systems, discourses that leach onto our libidos. The idea of toxic masculinity is the same mistake that the early, often male, psychoanalysts made when they desired a perfect powerful prohibiting father. Theory, like sexuality, is permeable to childhood fantasies of the proper protection of parents, especially in times as volatile as these. Male sexuality is, at its best, tragi-comically traumatic, a strange and alien creature that a body must host and accommodate. What a man can do with his body, what he can make of the inklings of a gratuitous pleasure only barely linked to procreation, needs to be given form – close to ritual passage, constraint and release, maximal play.

Let's turn to *Thalassa* by Ferenczi and the question of genitality. It seems the book is built on a ruse, the ruse of the temptation or desire to return to the womb, to water, as a principle of the death drive. It depicts the drive to return to inorganic origins, to death or Nirvana, as integral to the theory of genital sexuality. *Regressionszug* evokes in English the trait, pull, rift, and drift of regression. In this one seemingly simple term, an abyssal, contradictory and aporetic logic is at work, and all the terms involved in it are slippery like a fish. The logic of equivalences is confusing, as confusing as the logic in *Beyond the Pleasure Principle* (1920) where Freud must finally admit that the idea of a foundational division between life and death drives is simply a rhetorical trope, a false distinction: there is not pure Eros or Thanatos; rather they slip, like the death drive itself. Why would a return to sea, or even to the womb, to the confines of the mother, promise Nirvana?

This slippage – both 'on the surface' and 'in depth' – is emblematic for Ferenczi of the attempt to return to a state of bliss that becomes death manifest as 'catastrophe'. It doesn't take Ferenczi very long to land us on the shores, impose a forced evolution, a reproductive struggle, an ice age and a scorched earth: 'The possession of an organ of copulation, the development within the maternal womb, and the circumvention of the great danger of desiccation – these three terms thus form an indestructible biological unity which must constitute the ultimate basis of a symbolic identity of the womb with the sea and the earth on the one hand, and of the male member with the child and the fish on the other.'[3]

No psychoanalyst who has read this text can forget the analogy of the introjection of the sea inside as amniotic fluid and the semen/baby like a fish attempting to return home. For Ferenczi this condenses a whole history of phylogenetic catastrophes: the history of the earth in crisis that is present not only in every attempt at regression, but in every attempt at coitus, which he makes the hallmark of the progressive unification of the drives in genitality, though it is less a bliss than an act of anxiety-ridden violence – another hole, or forced water-pit marking an ever-increasing force of separation.

Forget breathing. Forget the inflow of air, the end of bisexuality in sexed reproduction. Forget that the origin of coitus is rape. Forget the creation of limbs in order to pin down the body of the other.

Let's go home to the sea where we are men and women both, where we simply release our bodily products into the fluid around us, wrap ourselves in ourselves and in an environment that is nourishing, wet, one. Let's forget that this oneness is only circumscribed in the act of fertilisation that essentially happens without us ever being there; neither parent is there, nor is the child.

Ferenczi dreamt up this book, maybe even hallucinated it, while working in a military hospital, filled with war-traumatised patients, but also with dismembered bodies. He writes about genital functioning:

According to the conception here presented, the pro-creative function thus concentrates a whole series of elements of pleasure and anxiety into a single act: the pleasure of liberation from disturbing stimuli of instinctual origin, the pleasure of return to the womb, the pleasure of happily accomplished birth; and the anxiety, on the other hand, which has been experienced in the course of birth and that which one would necessarily feel in connection with the (fantasied) return to the womb. Since the actual return is limited to the genital and its secretion, while the rest of the body can keep itself unscathed (and takes part in the regression 'hallucinatorily'), every element of anxiety is successfully eliminated in orgasm as the procreative act that terminates with a feeling of complete satisfaction.[4]

Complete satisfaction? How could the return to the womb be at once a happy pleasure and a scathing anxiety that returns us to every trauma, personal and geological, which must then be extinguished or 'conducted off' by orgasm? Ferenczi also calls this process a complete identification with: the genitals; the genital products; the desired baby (even though it is also a parasite); the fish that we once were. Identification produces the unification and organisation of the sexual drive, uniting the anarchy of infantile sexuality, without mature genitals. Here the book is at its most fantastic, and it undoes itself almost completely. Yet, this is its truth: there is no unity aside from a fantastical identification; unity of identification as libidinal process itself – and this is what has been called, for the longest time, the 'phallus'. This is the only theory of genitality we can have as analysts, one that Freud pointed to in his essay on 'The Dissolution of the Oedipus Complex' (1924) and that makes its appearance constantly in his letters to Ferenczi about Otto Rank, about what Freud thought was mistaken about the theory of birth trauma. The problem is always a problem with the phallus; and as it concerns genitality, Freud advocates not for the repression or triumphant assumption of the phallus, but for its total destruction, or 'dissolution' (*Untergang*, which means 'decline, destruction, end, ruin'). Maybe we could add to destruction Ferenczi's notion of genital catastrophe.

With this phallic fantasy, are we pointing to what Ferenczi tries to undo, time and time again, when he attempts to find a more feminine essence in his theory, with and against his love for Freud? Freud felt that Ferenczi was too feminine and needy, almost whiny, obsessed with having a child instead of working. Ferenczi was obsessed with having a child, caught in a complex sexual drama between mother and daughter patients, sleeping with both. A situation that Freud despaired of. One patient was coveted for her fertility, sexual passion and youth, and the other for her intellectual adventurousness, though he had a less passionate relationship with her, and she was unable to give him a child. Since the women seem to be pawns in his drama, we might speculate that the situation with Ferenczi and these two women is not really about the women themselves, nor about the baby, nor even the splitting of love and desire (despite its considerable presence as a theme), but about writing to Freud. Ferenczi seems to need to find his voice or his name, with and against this man that he loves, who is also his psychoanalyst.

Given that Ferenczi wants to account for the evolution of the human species, one might find it odd that the development – or rather 'event' – of language is nowhere explicitly included, which for Lacan is an experience that is catastrophic, a violent separation and alienation, even if it is structuring. This is why Lacan links the phallus and language.

It comes as no surprise that in the moment he is working on this book, he struggles with the question of writing. He is concerned to find a way not to write letters to Freud, or to make his work the means of conversing with him. Ferenczi writes to Freud on 13 May 1914: 'Stemming from the problem of enuresis [involuntary urination], some ideas have occurred to me about the "amphimixis of partial instincts" at the onset of the primacy of the genital zone. This time I set about not to dissipate the matter with epistolary and oral discourse, but to write the matter up and – without regard for possible disgrace – to send it to you as free associations on this theme.'[5] The task would take him another nine years.

During this time, he wants to have a child, and doesn't want to have child; he wants to write a book, and cannot write a book: what else is this than a problem of identification?

'Language' is not addressed but constantly put to use by Ferenczi, who was a prolific writer and inventor of terms and concepts. Imagine here a 'fourth narcissistic insult' that – after Galileo's, Darwin's and Freud's – Ferenczi would have administered to mankind by pointing out that 'intelligence' is not an inherent property or capacity, but has to be searched for and found 'in the cosmos', by leaving oneself, turning oneself outside. This intelligence is language which is also the most external. In fact, its very intrinsic nature is assigned to it by what is external to it. This is a feature that 'amphimixis' concretises in the genitals. They are nothing in and for themselves; even procreation is nothing in itself: they only serve the purpose of the return they never accomplish, the mixing of fluids, mixing of DNA, mixing of functions, with no unity or telos.

Furthermore, the term 'amphimixis', which Ferenczi claims as a neologism or terminological coinage of his very own making, and which is set into the title of *Thalassa*'s first chapter ('Amphimixis of Eroticisms in the Ejaculatory Act') makes one think of the '*Sprachverwirrung*' ('Confusion of Tongues'), the title of his famous late – and very controversial – essay. Both amphimixis and *Sprachverwirrung* are traumatic for thought: they hint at fundamental confusions inside language and inside the construction of bodies and reality. The concepts themselves (i.e. 'language', 'reality') remain deeply altered, traumatised, estranged from themselves, and maybe impossible to grasp. Both amphimixis and *Sprachverwirrung* render language and reality impossible, calling up the Real in Lacan's sense. Ferenczi might have been intuiting this dimension more than thinking it. He seems at any rate to shy away from exposing or saying explicitly what comes with these two – as well as other – traumatic notions in his own discourse and thought.

Incidentally, reflecting on his theory of genitality a decade later in his clinical diaries, Ferenczi radically differentiates himself from Freud. He writes,

The ease with which Freud sacrifices the interests of women in favour of male patients is striking. This is consistent with the unilaterally androphile orientation of his theory of sexuality. In this he was followed by almost all of his pupils, myself not excluded. My theory of genitality may have many good points, yet in its mode of presentation and its historical reconstruction it clings too closely to the words of the master; a new edition would mean complete rewriting.[6]

Ferenczi would then go on to wonder if a more feminine element of the death drive was overlooked by Freud; an element that, starting from a 'heterosexual direction of the drive' and an early 'knowledge of the vagina', would include self-sacrifice, selflessness, kindness even, and fragmentation, as opposed to egoism and self-assertion.[7] This finds its way into Ferenczi's work on trauma and traumatic fragmentation around the same time, when Freud writes him a letter lauding the work as 'ingenious' and on a par with his great work *Thalassa*. Ferenczi coolly replies that the theory is a practical addendum to the *Thalassa* work, and while he was pleased to be called 'ingenious', he would have preferred to have been called 'correct'.[8]

A Young Boy and His Mother

Jouissance is a psychoanalytic term that has grown increasingly obscure. It denotes certain addictive and immediate forms of enjoyment, enjoyment that is more pleasure than pain, enjoyment suffused with aggression, and in general, an enjoyment that is unbound, unlimited, that seeks the transgression of limits and boundaries. It is often paired with the notion of desire, which is thought of as a defence against *jouissance* to the extent that desire is born of lack and takes place through complex interpersonal and symptomatic configurations that are part of a process of signification. In fact, this is one thing we might say about desire, that it is articulated, complained about, spoken, while *jouissance* remains mute, and resists signification.

How does psychoanalysis treat the problem of *jouissance*? Well, one obvious answer is through forcing it into the narrow constraints of desire and signification. But you might well ask, how does one do that? I will venture a strange answer. One way we know we are on the right track is when the analysis becomes somewhat humorous, to both patient and analyst. Humour may very well be a treatment of *jouissance* which is often anything but funny, and in fact, quite tragic. While Freud once thought of humour as suffused with *jouissance* – with sexual and aggressive tension – he later felt that humour was subversive and has the power to challenge the super-ego which fuels *jouissance*.[1]

When I think about these moments of humour between patient and analyst, a series of sessions I had with a young boy of seventeen comes immediately to mind. There was a lot of laughter in these sessions, and afterwards, in reflection upon them. I smile when I think of this piece of work. But like the strange insularity of an analytic session, I wonder if this humour is at all communicable. Who thinks someone else's analysis is funny in the slightest? And doesn't the seriousness of psychoanalysis, the time and investment, preclude too much humour? Most interesting in this piece of analytic work is that here humour meets violence. Humour is found at the hinge of an encounter with one's own sadism, that sadism acting as a basis for the comedic action. The series of sessions move toward a kind of tipping point where humour from a more conservative defensive position moves toward something more radical.

What we will see is that a crucial element in the distinction between one form of humour and the other is an encounter with *jouissance* and its transformation into the desire of a subject. The subject, we might say, through this encounter, locates a new position, this new position appearing and announcing itself in the form of a laugh. Following this logic, we might say that *jouissance* without desire is anything but funny, and desire alone is not funny enough, tending more towards the tragic. Taken together, desire coupled with the intensity that *jouissance* lends to it through the register of the drive – repetition, the Real of the body, and that traumatic kernel beyond symbolisation – we have the setting for a possible humorous know-how with one's symptomatic comedy of everyday life.

A boy walks into an analyst's office.

Three years later, she forces him to write down his dreams spontaneously in a session in which he has played at telling and not telling, remembering and not remembering what he dreamt over the weekend. He had the following dream: 'I am in an old medical room, you know, like the ones you see in the pictures that they use for teaching, like they are round and there are bleachers where people watch. You know what I'm talking about. Yes? Well, it's there, and I can't see who is in the audience; it's all blurry anonymous faces, and I'm on an operating table, and you're there . . . and you're carving me like a turkey. Just removing huge chunks of me and putting them in a bucket, throwing them in there, piece after piece . . . You were just going at it! And everyone was watching. You sadist! Like it was nothing, just cutting away . . . and I don't want you to know how much it hurts.'

After much discussion of the dream – a dream he more or less interpreted himself with ease – I asked him if I was going at it because I didn't know that it hurt him. He had said that he hid it very well. He replied that he didn't know, but then asked me directly, 'Now that you do know, will you do anything differently?' I looked at him quizzically. 'Probably not,' he said, 'because you are so goddamn evil . . . That look on your face.'

'But, this was a lot of fun, more fun than I thought,' he added.

The dream had a profound impact on me. First of all, it was funny when he was telling it to me, playing at accusing me of being a sadist. Violence and humour mix with rapid force, a sardonic attack that stretches in both directions. In addition, and on a more touching side, this young man more or less re-imagined the primal scene of psychoanalysis: Charcot with the hysterics at the Salpêtrière, adding the element of cutting so important to Lacan. The analyst has probably always been a figure who demands a pound of flesh; the one whose desire is imagined to be a desire for something brutal. His appeal to me not to do anything differently in the face of his pain is certainly a desire he holds for himself, a wish to be able to sustain his desire.

Jouissance has the force of a transgressive violence in the dream, which served as a first link to a question about *jouissance* that he began to ask in the analysis. It is certainly also a response to my having displayed my desire as analyst, forcing him to bring me dreams. The weirdness of the analytic relationship is contained in the image of the turkey-carving in the amphitheatre, translating the untranslatable act of talking about dreams and about *jouissance*. Is a comedic undertone what allows this dream not simply to be a nightmare? Is this humour a problem? Is this a veil before the Real? Or, does it open the possibility of something else, perhaps something like sublimation?

He had another dream: 'I jack a car, pulling the driver from the driver's seat, get in, drive it recklessly, crash it, get out, and do it again. I jack another car, pull the driver out, drive it around the block, crash it, do it again . . . And then, guess what?' He looks at me. 'What?' I respond. He makes a well-timed pause. '. . . Well . . . I jack another car, pull the driver to the ground, get in, drive it around the block, crash it, I jack another car, pull the driver to the ground, get in, drive it around the block, crash it, and I do it again. And again, and again.' There was a joke in the dream about repetition, repetition itself a pivot between humour and its other side, brute tragedy. He allows this other side, and his fear to creep in: 'It felt like it went on forever, it felt like it would never stop.'

At a conference in Leuven in 1969, Lacan famously told the dream of a patient of his, who dreamt of an infinity of lives springing from herself in succession, a Pascalian dream of being engulfed in an infinity from which she awoke half-mad. As the audience burst into laughter, he assured them that while it might seem funny, it was not funny in the slightest to her. Repetition is madness incarnate and indeed this carjacking dream is mad. The 'endless, pointless, chaotic violence', as he put it, was a metaphor for his tie to his mother – a maddening masturbatory jacking-off game that they both shared and which neither could end. 'It ends when I pull her down with me,' he told me in a state of glee. 'I'm in this fight to the death. I've got it all mapped out.' And he did, it is true. He had been telling me the rules of the game for the past year.

The *jouissance* in this dream was even more palpable than the first. There in the sexual language – 'pull her down with me' – but also in the very rhythm of the dream, pulling one

off again and again and again. 'And you spare me such torture?' I asked him at one point. 'I don't think I can win against
you,' he quipped. This was not entirely true, since some game
of withholding was certainly at play: an obsessive strategy that
I took on by force, forcing him to tell me his dreams. It is not
a tactic I generally use, but something moved me to try and
break up a kind of deadly repetition. One lives through games
of *jouissance*, games that my patient managed to force (with
difficulty) into the intersubjective arena. I did him the service
of likewise forcing some of this into the arena or perhaps better, amphitheatre, of his psychoanalysis.

His satisfaction, from my perspective, was never totally
insular, although it could become so during earlier periodic
severe depressions and for periods in the analysis. Three
years into treatment, he could exude a new charm in certain
contexts in his life, in particular when he 'played games' with
his friends, with authority, and with girls. The game is something he loves to constantly renew, with greater and greater
demonic force, an upping of the stakes that he relishes. He
attributes, in the dream, this demonic force to me, the analyst, someone whom he sees as asking him to play every session. Every session feels like a renewal of a command. *What
are you going to talk about today? How far will we take this?* This
is how I would describe the particular exigency of his question that emerges in his analysis: *In what way can we play with
an elusive pleasure, always bordering on sadism, so that we aren't
just engaged in pointless repetition?*

After the carjacking dream, I pointed out to him that he
wanted his own car, that for the first time he would be in the
driver's seat if he got one, and that most of the fights with his
mother that I could remember took place with him in the
passenger seat, especially when she drove him to see me. 'I'm
going to carjack that bitch, pull her out of the driver's seat,'
he said with delight. He then told me that the car he picked
out turned out to be the same car his father had when he was
young, a Datsun. He didn't remember that. His mother told

him. I don't doubt that the 'Da' joined to the 'son' in the name of the car is coincidental. But then again, I wouldn't. And in any case, the name-of-the-father constantly circulates in this story; there even as the authority of the one who carves turkey on Thanksgiving. We are thankful that there is this third.

Is it always this iteration of an Oedipal story that is the force behind repetition – violent, incestuously sexual hilariousness? Does masturbatory *jouissance* always rear its head in a joke, the play of the punchline? What transformation makes repetition something humorous and not simply tragic? Sheer symptomatic repetition in treatments, as many of us know, feels lethal, and we perk up as the work of analysis mutates this repetition into something else. But the something else, at least as I'm thinking of it with this patient, is still repetition.

It brings to mind Lacan's early distinction between the repetition of a need and the need for repetition. The first he locates as a collapse of desire into interminable need and frustration, landing one in the stuck economy of the imaginary. The second – the need for repetition – is located more on the boundary between the symbolic and the real, the place where language brings itself to bear on one's desire life, forcing us into an interminable search for what is already lost. The drive is structured through repetition, but repetition always brings with it some difference. If we search time and again for the same lost object, turning around this hole, we nonetheless can find our self somewhere new and unexpected. The drive needs the force of repetition – transgressive, on the edge of violence, often flying in the face of reality – with which it carves a trajectory in the world. But it is not the aim in the end, which in any case is a kind of eternal return, if not encounter with a cause for renewal, but rather the way taken.[2] Not, I would say, the bitching in the car that happened over and over and over but the wild exclamation: 'Carjack that bitch!' It reminds me of Lacan's command, taken from the book of Revelation 10:9, to 'eat the book'. This command is not dissimilar from Lacan's ethical injunction: *Have you lived in conformity with the desire that is in you?*

Having linked desire to the lost object, the object eaten which can now be raised up, there is a kind of faith put in desire, in the hole in which it always escapes. And this is the work of repetition, infinite carjacking, but whose point is this acknowledged horizon of *jouissance*. *Jouissance* contains history, a history that is relived, repeated. One of my patient's main symptoms was kleptomania. The car he doesn't know that he infinitely steals, drives and crashes, is his father's. Far from this being a renunciation of a wish, the analysis brings about its demonic fulfilment.

He tells me another dream: 'I am at my grandparent's house and they tell me we have to hide this gun from my mother. I don't know why or what they are worried about. My mother comes in and gets me and tells me I have to go with her. We are in her car. I remember driving past an airport, I don't know how to explain it, but it was on stilts, or a second storey. She turned a corner and says, to me "I'm going to get pumped!" She takes me to a place called motherland where they take her motherstuff.'

'Motherstuff?' I ask.

'Yeah, well,' he says sheepishly, 'you know, babies and milk.'

'Oh, pumped,' I say.

'Yeah, I figured it out at that point.' We both start laughing as the look on his face seems to embody the slippage between pumped and pumped. He carries on: 'So there we were in motherland. I don't like it there. I really don't like it there. I want to leave. I go outside and there is a pack of zombies eating people. Their mouths are red around the edges, like when children are eating cherry popsicles.'

'Except it's blood?' I ask.

'Except its blood . . . Thank you. And the people are just disappearing, one by one. I run down the street and I stop. I look across the street and I see you inside a donut shop. Bright, yellow, and there you are, happy as Larry, just selling donuts, with a hat and an apron, the whole thing, all smiles, all donuts. Just like you always are, sitting inside this office.'

'Where I sell donuts?' I ask.

'Yup, you and your damn donuts', he says. 'So I'm wondering if I should go in there, your donut shop. It doesn't seem like a place to stay. I look down the street and I see this girl, you know the one I told you about' – a love interest – 'and she's walking into a church and I can't tell if it's another one of these places, vampire, motherland, lair where they pump you. Mother-pumper place. Or is it somewhere safe. Then I look down the street and the zombies appear and we meet eyes, which is bad, you know it's going to be bad when your eyes connect with a zombie's.'

'And then what?' I ask with anticipation.

'And then I disappear. I can't figure out in which direction to move.' He pauses. 'I'm sick of your donuts, I'm sick of my mother, I don't know about this girl, all the goddamn zombies. I'm sick of it all'.

Shouldn't we all breathe a sigh of relief: at least the analyst's donuts have a hole. If milk and babies and motherstuff are not entirely distinct from donuts, which also have a flair of the maternal about them, something to be sick of or sick on like the rest, the difference is in the structure! We have 'donut' on the one hand and 'pumped' on the other. Is it the impressive orality of the dream that brings this hole with it? Does the mother, losing her phallus (gun), lead to the unravelling of the pumping scene? Pumping certainly seemed like the decentred centre of the dream: a word that moves between aggression (pump a gun), excitement (pumped!), being depleted or parasitically vampirised (pumped), sexuality (pumping), and finally, hopefully more analytically, the draining of *jouissance*, the creation of a space of lack that we begin to see in the next iterations of the dream work. We analysts, one could say, not only make donuts, dough off of nutters, the selling of a no or a nothing: psychoanalysts are also mother-pumpers. Happy as Larry, a sump-pump, or the pimp of all pumps. I could really go on.

A week later he ran away from home. He re-enacted the end of the dream by literally disappearing. Far from a moment of the aphanisis of his desire, letting it slip away from him and disappear, in the act of running away he brought his desire forward. It was an impulsive act for sure, and he showed up to my donut shop-office, bag in tow with his favourite pillow that had never left his bed, and all his other things he might need, like his favourite DVDs, visibly weighing on his shoulder. But, he showed up, it must be said, to his regularly scheduled appointment.

This separation had two very interesting consequences. First, his mother decided after this event to get him a place to live separately from her while he finished high school – the fighting between them, she finally acknowledged, was too much and try though they might, neither could stop. Second – and this in part explained the airport in the dream – my patient had never really been away from his mother, not to go to camp, or on any other such occasion. He had gone to visit a friend in Buffalo to see what college life was like about two months before the sequence I'm telling you about. It was his first trip away (something I didn't know or didn't appreciate fully) and his mother drove him to the airport just like in the dream. He ended up stranded in Buffalo for a week longer than planned because of Hurricane Sandy.

He told me that he was miserable on this trip. He didn't know anyone, he didn't know where to go, he didn't know what to do, he had no clean clothes, slept in random places, the dorm bathrooms were filthy, and he just felt sick to himself and terrified of going to college. He had hoped that this trip would provide a point of relief from the awful year of failing in school and endlessly fighting with his mother. He was hoping that he would feel free. But it didn't feel that way. He hadn't told me this. He just came back and was listless and defeated.

'What didn't feel free?' I asked.

'Well,' he said, 'I was worried about what my mother was going to do if I wasn't there. I think I've always worried about that.'

'In what context?' I asked.

He detailed a history of her abusive relationship (she was the instigator) with a man he lived with from an early age. I knew about this, but I did not hear it like I heard it this time. 'That was more the problem, this worry, than just hating Buffalo, which is still a total shithole, don't get me wrong, but I think I was preoccupied by that, that and the friggin' storm or hurricane or whatever. Oh, yeah she had to pump out the basement which was flooded, don't say another word about that . . .' He continued, 'And the thing about running away was that I didn't do anything I don't normally do at home, but for once I wasn't doing them or not doing them because of her. I didn't care, somehow, about what she was doing; I think she'll probably be happier, and I think I used to feel that if she was miserable without me or happy without me, that I had somehow lost and she had won, you know the fight I'm having with her for eternity . . . I just didn't feel that way this time when I ran away.'

The analysis, of course, continues on, and the vicissitudes of turkey-carving, carjacking, popsicle cannibalism, stealing and pumping and disappearing, vampire lairs and the analyst's donuts, are not forgotten. Last week the donuts were on a conveyer belt and he was peeing on them. We spoke a great deal about active urethral *jouissance* as opposed to the passive brutality of erections.

What has changed from my perspective is that repetition in this treatment has a strikingly different character. It always comes with a bit of humour, with a lightness of touch. It has lost a certain fixity that the death drive can lend to it, unravelled in these sessions with the carjacking dream the high-point of its appearance. Humour, in the end, is not a negation of death or loss, or indeed of the seriousness of his (albeit sexual) rage towards his mother, it contains them in a rather passionate and comedic play. The body is there, as it is in so much of humour in its oral, anal and genital variants: the body in all its tragic-comedic glory and decay.

For my patient, his symptomatic relinquishing of desire and collapse into depressive revelling in *jouissance* becomes in these sessions instead a kind of driven know-how whose signature or stamp is the humorousness of sadistic momentum: carving, carjacking, crashing; pumping and peeing even. If there is an object of the drive, it is, in the end, the nothing of what the analyst offers, speech of course from one angle, but also the mother's body taken in and lost. This is different than the object of *jouissance*. The immediacy of contact and excitement and aggression of *jouissance* eclipses desire. It was as if the treatment transferred this impossible enjoyment into the content of the work and then allowed it to come undone, take a new form. In a sense, he gave it up in order to separate from his mother, a move I think that was signified by getting 'sick of it all' but also in figuring me as the woman in the donut shop – a place to go, maybe a place even to run away to, but not a place to stay.

Dream

Did you ever hear the joke, *Why is six afraid of seven? – Because seven ate nine*. I remembered it thinking of having to write this letter to you in December about November, not least because I'm afraid of counting backwards, especially this close to the end of the year. Seven already eight nine, and letters are difficult because they invite an encounter; I'm already uneasy on the precipice of this new year. Let the countdown start again at twenty and double down. So, I woke up today unable to open my eyes, as if they were caught at half mast, as if I was born to look at the ground. I spent a good part of the evening in a bad dream of the cruellest violence, staring down the tip of my nose, at the tip of a man's boot, just before it started kicking me (clearly I was working with the proximity of the letter b to the numeral 6). In that one short moment before the outbreak of violence, the stillness seemed to be a moment of prayer, not afraid of anything, not afraid of what seven had done to this year or to the next, just sitting quietly at six, praying, expectant, not seeing much, and not knowing anything of what was about to happen (6 looks like it's kneeling, doesn't it?). They say six is the pregnant number because of the way it looks, though many will associate it with nine – depends on your style, morphological or epistemological, or even mythological. I was kicked about nine times in the stomach, curled around myself in foetal position, either the mother losing her child, or the foetus in the mother, about to be lost herself, the way six and nine can wrap around each other (can you see – sixty-nine?), all of this trying to get me to the place where I could finally say what I wanted to say, which came to me as the word from the first page of a book I haven't read in so long, a book about writing (and answering) letters, Nathanael West's *Miss Lonelyhearts* (1933).

Soul of Miss L, glorify me.
Body of Miss L, nourish me.
Blood of Miss L, intoxicate me.
Tears of Miss L, wash me.
Oh good Miss L, excuse my plea,
And hide me in your heart,
And defend me from mine enemies.
Help me, Miss L, help me, help me.
In saecula saeculorum. Amen.[1]

The letters the agony aunt Miss Lonelyhearts receives torment him (he's a man); he doesn't know how you put anything out of its misery, can't find an answer to the cries for help from Desperate, Harold S., Catholic-mother, Brokenhearted, Broad-shoulders, Sick-of-it-all, Disillusioned-with-tubercular-husband, except perhaps to fight their misery with dreams. Letting such a thing stir in him, 'he knew now what this thing was – hysteria, a snake whose scales are tiny mirrors in which the dead world takes on a semblance of life. And how dead the world is . . . a world of doorknobs. He wondered if hysteria were really too steep a price to pay for bringing it to life'.[2] It's never too steep of a price in a world of doorknobs (8). Dreams bite and hurt, they are hysterical, they are pure body and the wish for body, unalloyed desire addressed to the other: glorify me, nourish and intoxicate me, wash me and hear my plea. I place myself on the ground in front of thee, on the altar of a new year. Bring me back to life. *Saecula saeculorum* (∞).

On the Ongoing Realities of Sexual Abuse

Questions of trauma and truth still haunt the history of psycho-analysis. Every case should bring what psychoanalysis thinks it knows into question.

Freud famously abandoned what he called the seduction theory of neurosis, deciding that sexual abuse wasn't the aeti-ological cause of neurosis. Abuse and various forms of trauma certainly made things worse – the violence takes centre stage in the same way obsessive thoughts can, or bodily suffering – but it wasn't required for neurotic illness to erupt.[1] Many have argued against Freud, whom they feel dropped the ball on exposing the harm caused by sexual abuse; I think he did expose it, including its prevalence, but his aim wasn't polit-ical or sociological, it was psychoanalytic. Freud wanted to understand the suffering of the psyche. He could not give a single causal explanation for neurotic suffering, and cer-tainly not one that depended on an external event in reality. Why not?

Psychoanalysis is interested in the subject, in what is singular to speaking subjects, and in what universal struc-tures delimit what is possible for humans, mainly because of sexuality. Psychoanalysis is interested in how it can inter-vene in this configuration. Like shell shock, which Freud also studied during the First World War, trauma overwhelms the psyche and forces something external to the front of the stage. But the question for any patient is, *What do you want?* Trauma buries the possibility of asking this question, Freud saw hysteria in particular as an important interrogation, but one that nonetheless continued to obscure the patient's desire.[2] Hysteria is a focus on the other to the detriment of the self, a focus on the other to the detriment of ever saying what you want.

Investigating human desire steered Freud more towards the world of fantasy, hidden enjoyments, and all of the ways we disavow responsibility for our *singular* truths. Attempting to speak in the direction of truth may be involved with the reality of sexual abuse; but it also may not be. Psychoanalysis, Freud says in a late essay on 'Constructions in Analysis' (1937), seeks only an element of historical truth, a kernel that touches on each patient's rejection of reality that leads to unreasonable expectations of the future.[3]

Freud diagnosed an ongoing war between the sexes in contemporary civilisation. He inveighed against our misunderstanding of childhood sexuality, and exposed the polymorphous nature of all human sexuality, wanting empathy for what was deemed, at the time, 'sexual perversion'. Freud worried that sexual morality was constricting sexual lives to the point of neurotic illness; he thought monogamy should be seen as a difficult constraint for men and women. He spoke out against the ridiculous fetishisation of women's chastity. And, in general, he felt that civilisation had to try harder to recognise the many and varied ways the psyche might organise pleasure and displeasure in human lives, and that the more we proscribe fixed programmes, fixed ideas around human sexuality, the more we court self-destruction as a species.[4]

Psychoanalysis places its work in the register of speech in a particular relationship of transference between doctor and patient. Every case is different and differently handled. Psychoanalysis moves a patient closer to an original traumatic kernel and all the fantasies, transgenerational truths, sexual conflicts, and affective explosions that encircle it. Freud thought of this work as bringing a patient closer to their hysteria, forcing the patient to lodge a complaint about the other and begin to reminisce as they moved closer to something that was, in today's idiom, triggering. He thus universalised hysteria as part of everyone's psyche, not just 'sick' women, equating hysteria with a search for a kernel of truth. Only through this encounter in a treatment did Freud feel that the trauma could give way to desire.[5]

Freud says that we must understand better how defence turned against a piece of the external world (hysteria) leaves the symptom and the personality intact, whereas the cost of the anxious structure is actually much greater. Anxiety isn't merely a negative force; rather, it is a question of a mass, a quantity, to which we must form a relationship. It demands palpable change in a system. Anxiety is constantly preoc-cupied by anxiety, it's unbelievably painful and boring, and desire is nowhere. It makes us live in a kind of medial zone of incessant defence and substitution, projection, denial and wishful thinking, what Freud eventually calls an unending series of half-measures. Anxiety arises in liminal spaces, in the sensation of oneself as a body with a foreign edge. Action, when based in anxiety, is reduced to controlling the appear-ance of this Otherness, either in oneself or the other person. Here we get a glimpse of why anxiety must be tied to sexual-ity, and why anxiety must give way to hysteria.[6]

I have lived through several 'hysterical' moments in which a patient has lapsed into a demand centred on trau-matic events or memories in their life. What is fascinating was that the demand was such that I was asked to do more than witness what was coming to the surface. I was being asked to act as a force of validation or verification, for example, of the patient as abused. In particular I was asked to condemn the acts of the abuser. These moments in treatment were incredi-bly difficult and volatile. To have to refuse to do so was almost unbearable and I was left with a lot of self-interrogation and doubt. Was abstinence in this case correct?

I felt some force of instrumentalisation of the trauma itself arising as a demand that I take up a role of authority that I had never otherwise assumed. This was an important stance for me as a psychoanalyst. Why this extreme demand for the analyst's presence suddenly in the treatment, I wondered? The patient appeared to disappear into the demand itself. She was lost to the treatment for this period of time. Her accusations became more and more paranoiac, by which I mean focused on the other as her persecutor, which started to also become myself. In no way did I prevent the patient from going to seek legal recourse, nor corroboration of the events with others, particularly family members. In no way did I deny the events as real. I just did not affirm that I knew with certainty that the patient was, in reality, abused.

Truth is not in my hands, nor even is it in the patient's hands from a psychoanalytic perspective. It is on the side of the act of speaking, and on the side of the unconscious, which only appears here and there, never in a full way. One could say that this demand was the purest resistance to the continuation of analysis itself. Given that this moment took place in a rather long psychoanalysis, it seemed to be about bringing the analysis to an end, recognising this last kernel of truth, her desire, repeating an original moment of trauma, making what counts not her own life, her own wishes, but something concerning the other.

A moment of paranoia in a case of hysteria

In the late stages of an analysis, close to termination, a patient started rehashing memories of violent encounters with her father. She was furious with him and wanted to punish him with her absence, with the erasure of his last name, and with showing herself as breaking certain codes of Jewishness. At the same time, she was beginning a relationship with a man who was quite different from her previous ones – much more satisfying. There was a question about getting married again, and having children – something she had forsworn.

A transitory symptom arose. She had a very powerful orgasm, one unlike others, she said, and it had led to some confusion during sex. She thought that he had removed the condom, or that it had broken and he hadn't told her. Even though this wasn't true – they checked – she then couldn't get the thought out of her head that he had lied to her somehow. She said she got the idea that he wanted to 'cut and run'. There was some feeling of him being too close, and yet also abandoning her, which terrified her and lay inside a feeling about him lying. Something was breaking.

Interestingly, she upped the ante on the wish that I would say that her father abused her. She recalled a difficult scene with him barging into the bathroom when she was a teenage girl, wrestling her in the shower. Was this physical abuse? Was there some sexual abuse that this memory was hiding? Or was it simply a moment that was too close? Inappropriate? Too over-excited? Could I just say what I thought this was? She was becoming more and more upset in session, saying that I was abusing her by not weighing in, and threatened to leave the analysis.

I wondered with her why this was coming up now; stated that we had gone over these memories many times, in previous years, without this demand upon me and intense rage. I also asked what this had to do with where her current relationship was at, and this question which had been foreclosed, of her wanting to have children. She knew that she felt absorbed by this paranoid feeling that both he and I were doing something to her that was embodied by this strange phrase – 'cut and run'. When she said it again, I heard 'cunt'. She said she felt that we wanted to get off on her, use her, get our rocks off, and discard her like trash.

The night after this session, she spilled very hot soup on her vagina. She was in the shower washing, crying, burned, as if to return to the scene with her father. Holding herself in the shower, she felt hatred for herself as a woman, thinking of herself as weak. She thought of the father inside of her, of her identification with him, at the same time that she was repudiating him, hating him for the power he had over her as a child. It is true that she returned to him again and again, or returned rather to her hatred of him and his imagined hatred of her – certainly a way of loving him. Maybe she would also like to 'cut and run'? What did this have to do with 'cunt'? The end of analysis was certainly beckoning.

What paranoia can teach us about the signifier 'he'

What is fascinating to Lacan about delusion or paranoia is that there is a fertile moment that becomes, for the psychotic person, a frightening fall into madness. In what composes the delusion, we can find certain elementary phenomena whose composition, motivation and thematisation have the same 'structuring force' as a whole and in their parts. There is a nucleus, a 'parasitic point' inside the personality, around which the subject constructs something that is 'destined to envelop and enclose it like a cyst, and, also, attempts to integrate it, explain it'. The delusion reproduces itself and therefore reproduces its own constitutive force, meaning that its structure is 'irreducible to anything other than itself'. It is this self-generative force that Lacan feels has been so profoundly misrecognised.[7]

Truth then, in the case of paranoia, is not hidden as it is in neurosis. The paranoia is provided with the elements of its own understanding, and in essence becomes a question of understanding – that it understands, how it understands, what it understands, meaning that meaning is referred to as such: 'What is the subject saying, specifically at a certain period of his delusion? That there is meaning. What meaning he doesn't know, but it comes to the foreground, it asserts itself, and for him its perfectly understandable.'[8] Even when what is understood can't entirely be articulated, it is clear that it is understood. You are always within the reach of understanding, and this is when illusion starts to emerge – 'since it's a question of understanding, we understand. Well, no, precisely not'.[9]

It is for this reason that much of Lacan's contribution to psychoanalytic praxis is 'against understanding' or oriented towards what he called 'non-knowledge'. All the tropes and idioms concerning the value of 'not-knowing' and 'tolerating ambiguity' file in here, but I think Lacan's point is more radical. The original synthesis of the ego, what we call primary narcissism, makes that ego an alter ego, makes the ego other. This alienation means that human desire is constructed around a centre which is the other in so far as it gives the subject unity, and the object is the object of the other's desire.

Once the subject is a speaking subject, this other becomes Other capital O, meaning that meaning is *also* alien – language being Other to us, something that is imposed upon us from the outside. If paranoiac knowledge is knowledge founded in an original egoic alienation, founded on the rivalry and jealousy of the symmetrical relation between other and other, ego and ego, it is only this third, the Other, language and the symbolic, that intervenes in order to overcome this rivalrous and competitive ground. 'Speech is always a pact, an agreement, people get on with one another, they agree – this is yours, this is mine, this is this, that is that.'[10] But the aggressive character of primitive competition leaves its mark on discourse.

Lacan points out that when Freud says that the paranoiac 'loves his delusion as himself', you cannot fail to hear the reference to the biblical command to 'Love thy neighbour as thyself', both in the sense of the pact and the rivalry that is just below the surface.[11] Indeed, it is the sentence *I (a man) love him (a man)* that comes to form the grammatical tenses of the psychoses for Freud – paranoia, where the verb is negated such that *I don't love him, I hate him, he hates me*, making up the persecutory phenomena; erotomania, where the object is negated, *I don't love him, I love her, she loves me*, marking the insistence of the eroto-manic delusion; delusional jealousy, where the subject is negated, *I don't love him, she loves him*, knowledge of motivations of the object of love; and finally megalomania, which negates the entire sentence, *I don't love him, I don't love anyone, I love only myself*. This last megalomaniac sentence, to a certain extent, is true of the entire structure of psychoses, which is why Freud called them, at one point, the narcissistic neuroses or narcissistic psychopathologies.[12]

While one might say that it is the narcissism, the delusion of grandeur, that is the most operative in the structure of the psychoses, Lacan is quick to make a subtle and necessary distinction. The problem really concerns the *he* of the *he hates me*, which Lacan says is a signifier, too primitive, that appears in the external world. What we are seeing is that 'in effect, this *he* is multiplied, neutralised, emptied, or so it seems, of subjectivity. The persecutory phenomenon takes on the character of indefinitely repeated signs, and the persecutor, to the extent that he is its support, is no longer anything more than the shadow of the persecutory object'. *He*, Lacan says, is the most primitive signifier. We have no idea what it signifies and because of this, it is (or has been), quite strong.[13]

This last statement is profound, not only because it bears in it the famous statement of Freud's regarding melancholia – 'the shadow of the object fell upon the ego'[14] – but it also indicates the axis around which the contemporary question we have about men, masculinity, the return of white supremacy from incels to Jordan Peterson to Trump, seems to turn, together with the counter-attack embodied in the #MeToo movement. The *he* is being multiplied, neutralised, *and* emptied of subjectivity. There is an attempt to render 'man' nothing, much as he becomes the 'sign' or 'shadow' of the persecutory object, the absolute subject. Man is considered at once synonymous with the substance granting of patriarchy and absolutely fragile, empty. There is an increasing insistence on the meaning of what a man is, despite the emptiness or stereotypy of these meanings.

Dora

As already noted briefly above, Lacan's analysis of Freud's
Dora turns around the question of her object of love that she
keeps carefully shrouded. It is famously Freud's misrecogni-
tion of who her true object of love is that led to the case's
failed cure and early termination. Lacan writes:

> The history, as you know, is that of a minuet for four
> characters, Dora, her father, Herr K and Frau K. Dora
> in fact uses Herr K as her ego, in that it is by means of
> him that she is effectively able to support her relation-
> ship with Frau K . . . It's only Herr K's mediation that
> enables Dora to sustain a bearable relationship. While
> this mediating fourth person is essential for maintain-
> ing the situation, this is not because the object of her
> affection is the same sex as herself [I (a woman) love her
> (a woman)], but because she has the most profoundly
> motivated relationship of identification and rivalry
> with her father, further motivated by the fact that the
> mother is a person completely obliterated in the paren-
> tal couple.[15]

This is how Lacan understands the instigating event that
led to a disequilibrium that developed into a persecutory syn-
drome with respect to Dora's father. It is the scene by the lake
when Herr K attempts to seduce her that is important – this
case runs like a #MeToo situation, with Herr K sexually coerc-
ing young housemaids, pressing his erect penis into Dora
when she was a young girl, threatening her and keeping the
keys to her room, and turning the tables on her, saying she
was an impure girl who would not have garnered his affec-
tion. We could see this not simply as a trauma or series of
traumas, but a trauma that is situated as a trauma by virtue
of a 'fertile' moment tied not to events, but in fact to Herr K's
saying to Dora, 'My wife means nothing to me.' 'Everything',

Lacan says, 'then happened as if she had answered to him – So, what can you be to me, then?'[16] The 'nothing' appears again. This time as something she sees coming from the man about women, to which Dora will make her reply: 'You are nothing to me.'

Dora, who had been complicit in the arrangement of this little quadrangle of people, suddenly began making demands, declaring that her father wanted to 'prostitute her and surrender her to Herr K in exchange for maintaining his ambiguous relation with the latter's wife'.[17] Freud even remarks that she herself understood that this was somewhat of an exaggeration, but that she could sometimes think of nothing else, including separating her father from his mistress. Freud calls this a supervalent thought designed to block out all others, designed to obscure the truth. This is important for understanding the kind of demands around allegations that can arise in a treatment.

Lacan's contention is that some kind of distance that had helped Dora collapsed, and her paranoiac thoughts were designed to re-establish a necessary distance. Sometimes this distance took actual form as compulsively running away from these three figures, at other times by dreaming of revenge against her father and separating him from his mistress, or, eventually, after taking some distance from the affairs, desiring to establish the 'truth' of what was taking place amongst the four parties, who didn't want to fully acknowledge what was going on.

The Freudian typography of the ego shows us how a hysteric, or an obsessional, uses his or her ego in order to raise the question, that is, precisely in order not to raise it. So what is the woman-hysteric asking? Her question is, *What is it to be a woman?* And in so far as she complains about men, or a man, it is because of an identification with him due to a fundamental dissymmetry in the paths of the little girl and the paths of the little boy with respect to the primary object – namely, the mother. But Lacan, who isn't going to give in to some kind of anatomical-gender essentialism, is quick to point out that what Freud is speaking about is not some asymmetry in reality, but with respect to the signifier.

Dora is wondering, *What is a woman?* She is attempting to symbolise the female organ as such:

> Her identification with the man, bearer of the penis, is for her on this occasion a means of approaching this definition that escapes her. She literally uses the penis as an imaginary instrument for apprehending what she hasn't succeeded in symbolizing . . . Becoming a woman and wondering what a woman is are two essentially different things. I would go even further – it's because one doesn't become one that one wonders and, up to a point, to wonder is the contrary of becoming one.[18]

Wondering may even mean not being able to become anything, especially when there is an insistence on finding certain symbolic co-ordinates for men, or a man, or fathers, or male leaders, in order to answer a question about one's own female sex.

Why? Because in the symbolic nothing explains creation, nothing explains life as such, and nothing explains sex, especially sexed reproduction – the signifier is incapable of providing an answer at any of these points or knots. One might suspect this is why Freud said that to wonder about the meaning of life is already to be neurotic. The signifier, essentially, signifies nothing, and the less it signifies, the more indestructible it is. In fact, the less it signifies the happier we are.

So where are we today with the question of the ongoing reality of sexual abuse? There is an emphasis on exposing the long-hidden truths of societies' double standards. But we are struggling to invent new ways to come together and restructure society, as the force of accusation, attack and counter-attack grows more and more intense. Can we hear a need for some kind of distance in this insistence on revealing the truth about others and never ourselves? Has the *I love him* been thrown into negation under a *He hates me*? What about the proliferation and emptying of signification around the *he*? The insistence on a question about others, sex, power, no doubt has profound effects, but it is also in danger of collapsing into an answer, a paranoiac answer, which arrives as an image of violence, presence, and thus the sheer negation of subjectivity.

Is then the question behind all of this (potentially hysterical, meaning it concerns a subject appearing at the intersection between sexuality and speaking truth) one that hides, even as it structures these detournements? Is this not present in these clinical examples at the point where the subject vanishes into a demand, where the most critical points of signification around what it is to be a woman, to be a sexual woman, and to love, and even desire men, or women, were precisely bringing themselves to bear? Psychoanalysis gives the answer, *Nothing, nothing real here, except what is Real*, namely, the figure of radical separation, the bare-bones reality of the truth of unending violence and confused sexuality in human civilisation, and the fact that we cannot signify what sex means, or life, or, for that matter, death. The question, reaching an intensity of insistence, a radical rejection of reality, is first an outbreak of persecutory supervalent actions and thought, and next – one can hope – a means to an end. Given that there is no answer, we have to invent something new at this degraded point (in human relations) that we have come to.

Useless Organs

In Paul B. Preciado's book *Can the Monster Speak?*, the text of a speech given to the annual conference of the École de la Cause Freudienne in Paris in 2019, psychoanalysis is lumped in with the psychological and psychiatric professions, the pill-pushers and mental hygienists, in order to make an appeal: 'I ardently appeal for a mutation in psychoanalysis, for the emergence of a mutant psychoanalysis, one equal to the paradigm shift we are experiencing . . . Perhaps this process of transformation alone, terrible and devastating as it may seem to you, now deserves the name of psychoanalysis.'[1] What deserves the name of psychoanalysis? Can we say what this mutant psychoanalysis could be, without drawing up a list of right and wrong, and without making excuses for anyone?

Preciado has a complicated relationship to psychoanalysis: at times understood by him as a high-bourgeois practice of domestication, a support and theoretical armature for normative visions of sexuality and gender, relying on outdated notions of interiority and the body as a private anatomical object grounded in binary codes. From a different perspective, Preciado flirts constantly with psychoanalysis: pointing to the importance of dreams during transitional moments in his life, the self-experimentation of Freud with substances and with auto-theoretical writing, the analytic chamber – which is often in the analyst's house – as a subversion of domestic space, as well as psychoanalysis's work with a new idea of the body as a somatic theatre, a living archive that is the site of radical transformation.

Preciado's 2013 book *Testo Junkie* served as a large part of the inspiration for my work on 'conversion disorder', in a book of the same name published in 2018.[2] Despite *Testo Junkie's* overt criticisms of psychoanalysis I found a way to read the work's formal aspects: the book as a process of mourning, a body-essay, an experimental protocol of intoxication, and a piece of self-analysis. I wanted to translate these aspects into the lens of the everyday practice of clinical psychoanalysis: looking at the way soma erupts in the consulting room, the conundrums of agency and identity and so many objects of frustrating satisfaction, the biopolitics of the psycho-pharmaco-pornographic era present in our symptoms, the unravelling and mutation necessary for paradigmatic shifts and epistemological rewrites, a longing for a future.

I wanted to consider the extreme limits one must traverse to locate an experience of desire, beneath or beyond the apparatuses of the state – something that Preciado narrates in his own life, with his own body, to show the state as penetrating further into our lives and bodies than many of us are prepared to acknowledge. His book functioned as a cut, a memento mori, that opened onto a desire pushing back against well-worn forms of control. This desire would be, in this sense, connected to an older regime, a pathological psychoanalysis – it can't really escape this completely, but as a transformation of it, it seeks to extract the more revolutionary path.

Preciado tells us that 'a philosophy that doesn't use the body as an active platform of technovital transformation is spinning in neutral. Ideas aren't enough'[3] – thus turning away from ideas and impotent epistemologies to soma, the theatre of the body, materiality and force, in a search for practices. Psychoanalysis as one such practice, in *Testo Junkie* in particular, is seen as a trafficking in substances between analyst and patient. The words exchanged have real effects in the body; psychoanalysis cannot leave behind this odd fact: that words impact bodies. This was one of its most radical discoveries. Preciado sees psychoanalysis as learning to live in somatic and semiotic environments that are growing more and more toxic. This is psychoanalysis not as simply modern – stuck in a turn of the century, syphilitic conception of the sexual subject as an interior – but brought into the contemporary moment which is only beginning to shift us away from this obsolete epistemology of interiority.

> Freud was a *cloaca maxima*, a sewer mouth who absorbed all the substances and techniques of the self, produced in his time. Inhaling everything that passed by, he would not spare any exposed cell, neither his nor others'. Therefore, it would be erroneous to say that Freud's psychoanalysis had uniquely, and as a matter of priority, been a treatment technique based on words. The distinctive feature of the Freudian sewer mouth was the ingesting of all the somato-semiotic techniques, incorporating all prostheses of his era and transforming them into living bodies and cultural discourse.[4]

What is the contemporary moment for Preciado? Preciado conceives of the body as taking on different epistemic frameworks, from the religious vessel for the soul to the museum of anatomical organs for the scientific gaze. The contemporary body follows the subject situated as more and more of an interior by institutions that bound that interior – from domestic life and the family, to mores concerning gender and sex, and government control via confinement and other forms of domination. But this interiorised body is growing outdated in our new global environment. Where this will go is unclear, but it is important to see that we are in a 'metamorphosis'.[5] Subjects are not controlled from the outside-in anymore, but rather the inside-out, much as the collective conscience is in the process of being externalised through technology. We are producing a multitude of prosthetic selves, new organs, open to contamination, rewiring and mutation.

Where will psychoanalysis fit into this? Preciado says of psychoanalysis, addressing me directly in an interview regarding its future:

I've been trying to think about what my problem with psychoanalysis is, and I think it's the power position that psychoanalysis has had about the interiority of the subject – a sort of monopoly over dreams and imagination, and an obsession with the family plot. It's not so much about doing away with this power but more the idea that psychoanalysis is at odds with reality now, with what's shifting. So can it work the same way? I say this, and yet I want what I call a 'mutant psychoanalysis', not a quest for interiority but a space for collective transformation of consciousness. I have so many questions, and Jamieson – you and I should talk – I don't think you're representative of the kind of psychoanalysis that's practiced.[6]

There is so much desire for psychoanalysis to be the locus for collective transformation. I understand this desire, wanting psychoanalytic change to function beyond the one-to-one relationship, our impotent work patient by patient. I have doubts that it can be more than this without degenerating into cultish control, without losing the intensity that time and singular listening creates, necessary for true transformation.

Preciado claims that the problem is that the relationship between psychoanalysis and this new reality feels increasingly at odds. Are the nuclear family and gender difference intrinsic to psychoanalysis and its clinical practice? Is psychoanalysis spinning in neutral? It's difficult to see who would have to be the one to truly find out, Preciado or the 'analysts'. Must Preciado be left alone with an analyst, one on one, in *their* chambers? Or can it be more collective, can they hit the streets together, can the analyst come to Preciado? Does he *really* want that?

This mirrors feelings Preciado has about a home, which he feels is insufficiently studied and perhaps cannot be a place for growth or realisation. The analyst's consulting room in their domicile is a fold in a home, as it was for Freud and

Virginia Woolf. More and more, however, for Preciado, this fold is not a revolution of domestic life and control, but a privatisation of the patient's life:

> In both cases – in the feminist struggle for a room of one's own as a quest for an interiority not defined by heteronormative demands, and in psychoanalysis as a practice of exploration (or creation) of the patient's interiority (an interiority that can also be called the unconscious) – to invent dissident cultural practices means also to invent new spaces, or to inhabit traditional spaces differently . . . This is why I'm so interested in a shift that took place after World War II: the relocation into the house of activities of economic production that were traditionally placed outside the domestic realm.[7]

But why is psychoanalysis seen here as a privatisation and interiorisation of the patient, rather than its own subversion of space? The patient gives themselves over to the somatic theatre of transference, much as Freud saw the symptom extending into the analyst's office, rearranging the usual order and rhythm of conscious-unconscious life. He called this the 'architecture of hysteria', which is a doubling of an interior architecture into the outside of the analytic process and ritual.[8]

Psychoanalytic offices are strange liminal zones, transitional spaces, belonging to both patient and analyst, and also belonging to neither. I love the theatre of my office and what takes place in the space of the waiting room, the bathroom, the entrance and exit. Why can't psychoanalysis be seen as the production of new forms of exteriority, for example, like that of dreams, symptoms, even acting-out? These certainly don't exist inside. Nor does transference, which is a fascinating externality, as well as speech or discourse. I'm not even sure it is psychoanalysis that produces interiority, though I agree that versions of it do nothing to help.

More than this, the power of psychoanalysis in general

is debateable. I find the marginal position of psychoanalysis comforting. It really only took centre stage for a short moment mid-century when the psychiatrist-psychoanalysts in New York – going against Freud's recommendations that psychoanalysis not be allied to medicine (Freud even sent Ferenczi to speak to A.A. Brill, who ignored them) – had power within hospitals and culturally (the same would be true of Lacanians in France). But even in this brief moment of psychoanalysis's heyday, the field quickly grew chaotic, dissolving into different factions, being left in the wake of the successes of CBT and psychopharmacology.

In the end, psychoanalysis became so much more strange and piecemeal. The presence of psychoanalysis in culture, both mainstream and highbrow, is infinitely perturbing, as if it were a virus that cannot be stopped even when there is a cohesive negative consensus against it. Preciado must admire this force, this swift infiltration, this adaptation. One cannot help but hear Freud's apocryphal story about psychoanalysis as a plague.

I don't know if I am or am not representative of the kind of psychoanalysis that is practised, nor whether I should be seen as an exception to any rule. But I can identify with what Preciado calls 'the axiom of the lamb' or the 'principle of the auto-guinea pig'. The analyst's experiments on themselves and the allowance for the other to use them, lend themselves to a struggle between life and death:

> The objective of the lamb: to struggle against the privatization of the body and reduction of *potentia gaudendi* to a workforce, a brand, a copyright, and a sealed biocode. The mode of functioning of the lamb: the pirating of hormones, texts, body techniques, knowledge practices, codes, pleasures, fluxes, chemical substances, cartographies . . . The transformation of the body of the multitude into an open living political archive: the common *somathèque*.[9]

I would tell Preciado about how the analyst tests everything on themselves first, allows the patient to pirate from them what they need. I want to explain how psychoanalysis is a body technique, writing a collective archive of bodies in a struggle against repression. I want to show Preciado how I live every day in my office with patients in complete flux, holding onto cartographies that are yet to be written. That in order to do this, I have to develop all manner of knowledge practices, knowledges that are open, living and embodied. My work is always in danger of closing down; in fact it will. This is my only guarantee.

Psychoanalysis and mourning are the paradoxical coming to terms with the useless organs that we carry around, that we never needed, but that were usurped nonetheless, or organs that we never even had and yet we still need to find a way to lose. It is about a process of separation based on a final disenchantment with representation ('ideas aren't enough'), a parting of ways with the desire for salvation ('no one will be able to do anything for my happiness'), in order to accept living in constant crisis. Psychoanalysis is testifying to this, to a life, finally, of ethical resistance, as a trace of a cut, where you test the one, you break it in half.

There are patients, who, right off the bat, exist as incessant crisis rather than in its covering-over; whose way of being seems to testify to this impossible bifurcation of life that renders everything arbitrary. They come looking for the place that Preciado is looking for, 'where desire really emerges', and they know it is only at the limit and have their eyes fixed on this outer edge. They engage in the fight for an impossible agency, an agency heretofore unknown but an agency that always, eventually, undoes itself, especially in the tumultuous vicissitudes of dependency, the commitment to crisis. These patients will test every aspect of your identity, and your identifications, because they cover over the place where your desire emerges. And if it is closed, if your being is sealed in this way, how can you ever help them with their project, with this search?

Sometimes these extreme practices go away as an analysis progresses and the patient looks suddenly neurotic: self-conscious; overcritical; emergence of a harsh super-ego; a need to be productive, efficient, a good girl or boy, live by a schedule, wake up on time, join the rest of the world . . . and I feel morbidly guilty. What have I done? You were so much more interesting before you started talking to me. And then I think twice about everything: I was so much more interesting before I became a psychoanalyst.

There are other patients I'd like to tell Preciado about – women especially who are confused about what their gynaecologists told them at twelve or fourteen or twenty-five or forty: about their periods being 'irregular'; that they don't have ova, only cysts; that they have too much testosterone, or not enough oestrogen; that birth control is the only solution; that they'll be in pain; that they'll be moody without it; that they'll, God forbid, get pregnant; that abortions will only further the problem, or solve it; that machines can explain to them the destiny of their femininity; that medicines and technologies will help them become pregnant at the exact moment that they want to; or, at the very least, that all of this will streamline an otherwise messy being.

These women often feel as if they have never known their own bodies, stuck in a fantasy of what was, or might be, having always lived with a body mediated by drugs. It feels impossible to know the difference between these medications and their body, these medications and the strange admixture that is fantasy and subjectivity. Impossible to find some demarcating line in a system that makes body, subject and object indistinguishable. My patients seem terrified of losing this pharma-object that stands between them and their bodies, leaving the question of gender, or indeed desire, in a state of suspension.

Some psychoanalysts tell me this is simply the mechan-
ics of fantasy: *It's birth control – what's the problem?* These
pharma-objects become more than what they are because
they are neurotic. It's the same when patients tell you about
the side effects of their antidepressants. You take it, it helps,
or it doesn't. I'm the one who participates in their fantasy of
what this is doing to their subjectivity, to their bodies. Their
subjectivity should be outside or beyond what are simply
the tools of an age. How can we argue against birth control?
Antidepressants have saved a lot of lives. Isn't subjectivity
always implicated in technology? The Greek techne shows us
this link between art, artifice, technology, being and politics.
It's as old as civilisation. I'm clearly hysterical. Searching for
some yesterday, some purity, some a priori being, that never
was. But, oh my God, all the people on psychopharmacolog-
ical medications, it's overwhelming. I'm secretly devastated.
I find a relief in Preciado's descriptions of this regimen that
infiltrates our bodies, and although it is a crisis, Preciado reads
forward, jumping into the future: gender has never been more
abstract, reality has never been more liquid. We should live as
if in end times; form ourselves as a point of the greatest tension in what Preciado calls a general 'cartography of extinc-
tion'. We cannot go backwards. We can only move forwards.

Many people I meet who watch pornography, who cannot find a way to stop masturbating, who buttress their sense
of identity and contain all that anxiety through a daily ritual-
istic consumption of sex, mirror these women and their pills.
It feels to me as if it doesn't matter what is said about the pornography in session – endless detail of what's watched, the
orifices, the cum-shots, the trolling of Craigslist escapades or
escort service ads – or, if not said, it will always be the blind
spot in a day, there in its silence, like the black space between
dreams and grocery lists. I cannot locate a desire in this stream
of images, in this bare life. I know I'm supposed to. But from
my end, it feels as if it needs to break or fall away or both.
Preciado tells me I'm in an absolutely new era: the production

of neo-non-subjectivities via frustrating satisfaction, a whole network of masturbatory co-operation, penetrable bodies.

What unites these patients in the light of Preciado's work is the necessity for a cut, a break in this chain, the reflexive loop, an incessant stream of being. He is right: 'Ideas aren't enough.' It feels as if it is becoming harder and harder to create something in this order of effect. As analysts, we should see that we are working against an immense system – the state penetrates deeper and deeper into our biology. Our act, if it is an act that works against this, would be radical. Its radicalism veers on terrorism, mirroring the trauma it seeks to transform because the act has the character of a shattering, ingested by the patient, rupturing, breaking in. Preciado sees transference love as a hyperproduction of 'affects', a 'prosthetic system of psycho-somatic information', 'a cybernetics of addiction'.[10]

Many contemporary psychoanalysts see the cure as an attempt at transforming what is understood as a symptomatic conversion in the direction of the body back into memory or into a representational frame, in the name of homeostasis. Theoretically this can be seen as a reassertion of the old categories of sexual difference and identity in conformity with pre-established norms. This is psychoanalysis as therapy or therapeutic. Freud was hypervigilant and violent in the face of any of his disciples who sought these kinds of changes, which he called their *furor sanandi*, their 'rage to cure'.[11]

Psychoanalysts, with their 'technovital' transformation, use and risk mutation in their 'cure'. If Preciado is (or isn't) concerned with the power of the psychoanalyst, in this somatic vision of Freud, the psychoanalyst is not in control of that which it tries to access. Its 'tools' are tools for mutants and mutations. Seeing psychoanalysis this way would be more radical than turning psychoanalysis into an epistemology (even when it is an 'anti'-epistemology of unknowingness), or a theory applicable to this or that academic discipline, or simply the degraded form of 'psychological accounts' that has emerged from psychiatry and the empire of therapies. Instead – and this is where my thinking took root – let's think of psychoanalysis as conversion disorder, as the hyper-production of somatic compliance as somatic invitation which solicits you, and solicits the new.

The psychoanalyst is the one who sustains the patient's test, sustains the testimony, allowing the patient to test the one, test their identifications, through them. The analyst's interpretations cut into these knots, as in surgery. These practices are uncannily condensed into the name 'testosterone'. Psychoanalysis and testosterone are two master signifiers that circle one another.

Together, psychoanalysis and testosterone aim at what Preciado calls the search for a body, sometimes one's own, sometimes another's, through an addiction that is the use of and play with an object that will never desire you back so that you can know your desire in its purity, reconfigure reality, self-legislate consumption, and arouse the most intense affects as lines or rifts of vulnerability. The psychoanalyst is the skin that comes to absorb these toxins, the locus for these fluids and their mutation, the space for mourning a body's useless organs in the exteriorisation and mediation of the subject.

Like Preciado, one can find in Freud the imperative to never travel backwards, only forwards. The agenda is the agenda of the 'symptom' that Freud says is looking for its 'own' end, its own telos.[12] We need to push this conversion as far as it will go, forwards, into unknown gains and surplus, to harness the power of this parasitic, irresolvable innervation. Psychoanalysis is not de-conversion, but the most radical conversion, which is another name for mutation. Psychoanalysis is a somato-militant vision which can be seen in Freud sticking to the strange language of the body and refusing to translate it out into more acceptable terminology and psychological categories: oral and anal phases, the phallus, genital and pre-genital sexuality, polymorphous perversion, castration anxiety, the repudiation of femininity, the pleasure principle, the death drive. This militancy and somato-terminological invention reverberates in the space between Freud and Preciado.

Sex Panic

Even as panic is one of the most isolated, internal and extreme individual experiences of fear, it is also completely contagious. I started to dream of panic night after night, perhaps in order to write this text, panic making a joke of itself even as the experience was anything but funny. The dreams left me so tired.

In the first dream, a few weeks ago, I was staring at a horde of animals, their beating feet ploughing through the earth as they crossed vast terrains of fecund nature, not pastoral nature, but nature that is primal, death-bound. Why is this image so anxiety-inducing, as if it mimics the racing of one's heart, the sound of a body meeting with the earth? It's also an image of war. I then find myself in some building opening a door to Anna Wintour and that cold stare of hers; her name a reference to the winter zombie apocalypse in the much-anticipated season finale of *Game of Thrones*. Wintour enters the room and inspects me like an insect, only to turn to the carpet which captured her ire more than I did, she then belting out to the staff the inadequacy of what she found herself standing upon. Why isn't she anxious? Why isn't this inspection of hers a sign of her own panic rather than her power? Isn't it?

Suddenly, my boyfriend and I are sitting together in the office of the principal, two chairs lined up before her desk – I never sit in front of people who sit at desks – and it's all rather unclear who is in trouble: our child, or ourselves. We are too old, he reminded me in the morning, to feel in trouble; we are, but you are never too old for this kind of panic, or at least not too old for the memory of it.

Next dream: I was beset by an image of garbage-filled seas, and was watching the last penguins on earth – somehow that's made clear to me – their little black and white bodies being bashed by the waves, or, having had a last joyous moment in the ocean, now being washed up on shore. 'They will not return,' someone says to me. This whole dream is some elaboration of a meme I saw on Instagram before going to bed where a woman hands a man a fish, and he asks for a plastic bag, and she says, 'It's already inside.' The caption for this particular meme was: *This meme just shit on the entire planet.* Or was it, *This is a meme of how we shit on the entire planet?* Forced to waste more time and go look it up – no, it was the first. What does that even mean – *This meme just shit on the entire planet?* I think my unconscious was interested in what the fishmonger said: *It's already inside.*

The dream comes to an end with an image of the purest anxiety – the transformation of something into nothing, pure diffusion or dissolution. The bodies of the penguins evaporate into a black and white substance, something that can now come out of a pen, ink on paper, the image producing some kind of a sonogram, some indication of what is on the inside – a pregnancy fantasy to be sure, but also a joke much better than the Instagram one simply because it's an unconscious joke on me about penguins, pens, penis, 'penic' as in having to write or give birth to this text on panic. The etymology of 'pen' is 'to add, to weigh, to weave'. In other words, another name for Webster. I gave birth to my own fucking name.

For Freud, pregnancy meant giving oneself over to the needs of the species, sacrificing one's individuality, inviting the reality of death; you become an appendage to your own creation, which, in any case, is going to leave you, will most likely survive you.[1] Procreation is division, evaporation. It's the opposite image to that of pollution where we claim the earth as ours, ours to shit on, as we imagine that we will survive it. Internalisation is both a figure of pregnancy and a psychic achievement – take it inside in order to get out of yourself.

*

The origin of panic is the god Pan, the wild satyr, half animal, half man. What is now called panic disorder – or its singular manifestation known as a panic attack – used to be called either 'anxiety neurosis' (a Freudian term which meant you were more anxious than neurotic and included, for Freud, the phobias), or, to go back even further, to the fifth century, 'pantophobia', which means the fear of everything, or 'vain fear', *inanis metus* in Latin.

This fear of everything is set against specific phobias, like of snakes or spiders or driving or flying or people, in psychoanalysis, because one is much better off when this everything can be reduced to a few things. Life is simply easier – just don't drive or fly or get near spiders or snakes or people. This was an important psychoanalytic distinction, because to be afraid of one thing gave you symbolic ground, whereas being afraid of everything left one no entry point to psychoanalyse. Nevertheless, phobia demonstrates that every symbol, every object, is simply a fixation. Panic demonstrates the way in which a mind can float, fixating on a negligible passing object, only to move to the next. It says something about the drift or drive present in anxiety and the accidental, fabricated nature of what occupies our fears.

Interestingly, this fear of 'all' covers over the origin of panic. It isn't in the 'all' meaning of 'pan', but refers specifically to the god Pan. This confusion between all as pan and Pan the half-man half-goat god is apparently the crux of several of Plato's jokes. Pan is wild; standing for nature as opposed to laws of the city. He was always depicted as virile: he taught shepherds to masturbate, had a constant erection, sometimes had sex with animals. Pan-sexuality is not only being blind to gender, but species as well. He was constantly raping or 'seducing' women, though these stories often end in failure and are mostly thought of as comical tales. Several of the women whom Pan attempted to rape escaped his wrath by becoming flora. One became a tree, another reeds on the shore of the river she ran across in in order to escape him. These reeds became the pipe he's often shown playing.

Women in panic become trees become sound. Sound becomes Pan's instrument of panic. The god was said to rustle bushes when people were travelling through the woods from city to city in order to induce panic. In the rigorous logic of myth, Pan plays with the foliage that represents the panic of almost-raped women in order to terrify passers-by as they step across the border that delineates man from nature, civ-ilisation from wilderness. Why, you might ask? Well, Pan doesn't like to be woken from his nap. It's when he's woken that he plays this game with bushes, or lets out a noise that induces blood-curdling fear. Hence the term panic.

In the seventeenth century, what was known as *panopho-bia hysterica*, also called 'panic terror caused by vapours', was described as the experience of sudden fright with dramatic reactions of racing heart or 'pallor' when startled by 'innoc-uous noises or sights' – caused by 'vapours', nothing. These vapours were then literally blown into women's vaginas as a treatment, to put their fears back in their proper place, namely, on the inside. While we are back to the theme of pregnancy, the question of worry, wild sexuality and noises that induce panic raises to my perverse psychoanalytic mind the question of the primal scene.

In other words, the noises that wake you from sleep, what you might stumble upon that is usually hidden, this induction into the reality of sex, especially as an infantile confusion about sexual pleasure and sexual violence, and the confusion that is the question of how and why babies are made. These noises you hear, this rustling in the bushes, are also the sign of what you are excluded from, what the others are doing and subject-ing you to, forcing you to be its witness. The imagination of the primal scene includes the attempt to be where you were excluded, to be present at the conditions of your coming into existence, the moment before you were, or the last moment when you were not. This is one way of thinking about incest – the attempt to breach the barrier of the specific conditions of your existence, not just your mother's vagina, or whatever.

Melanie Klein thought of the primal scene as an infantile fantasy of 'perpetual parental intercourse' and 'permanent pregnancy'.[2] Your parents are just constantly fucking and wanting more children. They don't stop. You have to listen to it night after night after night, contemplating the disruption siblings will potentially present to your life, especially your life at the centre.

Life in the primal scene is a permanent emergency, a panopticon – seeing all, hearing all, having it invade you, seduce you, hold you riveted to this all-ness, all at once. Unlike speaking or reading, which have to be parsed out, seeing and hearing have this quality of all-at-once – you have to keep listening to me to figure out what I'm saying, or not saying, have to read these words as they form a sentence that completes itself in order to find its meaning. The image I present to you, the sound of my voice, is something else. It's something that invades you.

Don't you think that this is what is happening on social media? Panic at the phantasmagoria of everyone in permanent procreation and production? Is sex panic not the reality of all panic, panic as making itself the witness to the excessive violence and enjoyment of others without mitigation?

For better and for worse, language given over to this immateriality, unmoored from objects and reality, is close to what some call our 'post-truth' world. And even if this post-truth world means existing in a state of deep panic – sometimes delusion – this would also be a world more delirious, poetic and comical. I do believe this. I'm a structuralist Lacanian. The drift of panic and anxiety puts us into the drift of language, which is always where poetry and humour find their home, or rather, their homelessness.

It may be the one shred of hope that I have – prose and humour – which I see everywhere around me, beyond primal scene fanaticism and its panicked adherents. I do think communities are forming on these fault lines, in the contagion of panic, even as they may seek to escape it. Either way, some truth about the real state of affairs is becoming clear; Freud always wondered if we had to become this sick to get close to a truth of this kind.

Pan is said to be the first and only god from the Greco-Roman Pantheon who dies. Some speculate that this is why Pan is probably the model for Satan. One might wonder about this encounter with wild sexuality and panic, followed by the death of god, occurring, or so it is said by Plutarch, in order to announce the transition from the ancient to the Christian world. So panic isn't just about perpetual sex you imagine others are having, nor is it solely about psychotic objects, it is also these as pointing to your death. Fantasy is always a last stop before the reality of mortality, utter helplessness, the fact that no one has what they need really, and no one can help you with the reality of death. When you are dead you will not know you are dead, you may only know that you are dying. The only omnipotent figure then is death itself.

Uncanny Sexualities

I seem like someone who is an expert on the clinical entity 'conversion disorder', having published a book under this title in 2018; though, truth be told, I was taking the diagnosis less literally and looking broadly at the history of the term 'conversion', playing with it as a synonym for hysteria, and using it as a prop for discussing the body in psychoanalysis. So, of course, I was referred the most extreme case of the diagnosis I had ever seen or heard of, a woman who presented with two years of increasing symptoms such as bodily states of paralysis and strange feelings in her flesh, major disruptions to her state of consciousness from feelings of intense derealisation (almost a feeling of not being in the world) to moments of amnesia, hallucinatory impressions and sensations (many of which took the form of felt presences) – all of which, as I'm sure you can imagine, led her to feel that she was going mad.

After countless visits to the emergency room and neurological specialists and other medical specialists, no organic cause was revealed. At one point, she had to move back home, her mother sleeping with her in her childhood bed because she was in such a state of terror. She got in a fight with the psychiatrist she was urged to see over a question of medication, and angrily sought a referral from a friend. After seeing her the first time, I thought she should find the real expert on conversion disorder.

The main features of her symptoms constellated around the theme of the uncanny, which was surprising since bodily conversion symptoms rarely feel so haunted. One might imagine that any disruption in the state of consciousness, any hallucinatory experience or set of strange bodily sensations, would have an uncanny quality. But this would be to make the mistake that Freud says we ought not to make regarding the specificity of the uncanny. A specific symptomatic condensation needs to take place in order to produce an uncanny effect, here, where the most material of symptoms – things that concretely happen on the level of the body and the realm of the sensory – are lined by the abstract qualities of uncanniness, an unease and uncertainty about a ghostly border of life, the body itself becoming a double, a harbinger of death.

This quality of uncanny conversion seems to have an irremediable effect on the sense of reality, one's place in relation to it, especially with respect to what can be known or said, and how this reality is tied to the symbolic or to questions of representation. The uncanny seems to be a psychosis that is somehow not psychosis, because the experience seems to have a representational quality to it, which makes it uncertain. I'll talk about how these qualities unfolded in this case, then speak briefly about a patient of Lacan who seems to have the exact reverse co-ordinates to this uncanny conversion disorder. I'd like to posit it as an uncanny 'cure', which involves, of all things, falling in love with reality.

In a perusal of the psychoanalytic literature I was curious about whether anyone had worked on the 'uncanny' as a clinical phenomenon. The only thorough paper is from 1934, from the infamous Austrian psychoanalyst Edmund Bergler. He writes:

> In the sense of the uncanny we take alarm at our own omnipotence, which for a few seconds we imagine to exist . . . The sense of the uncanny would thus represent a trance of a few seconds' duration, perhaps a brief state of mental alienation, and, from the standpoint of the ego, it is a *protective mechanism*. Dread of oneself (one's unconscious aggressive tendency) combined with dread of others (castration) result in what we might call an affective short-circuit . . . [and] the mechanism

serves the purposes of the super-ego at whose behest the feeble ego gives the danger-signal. Further, I would point out that the feeling of the uncanny may be secondarily *enjoyed as anxiety-pleasure [Angstlust]*, and masochistically induced over and over again ('sexualisation of anxiety'). This would at the same time serve as a gratification of the death-instinct in *dosi refracta*.[1]

Bergler feels that the uncanny is an overcoming of castration anxiety, an experience of a trace of infantile omnipotence that returns on the outside. It represents a sexualisation of anxiety, a masochistic submission to one's own split-off omnipotence. He goes on to elucidate thirteen ways we encounter this uncanny return of repressed omnipotence in patients. I'll summarise:

1) We may experience a sense of the uncanny when we watch another person giving play to his aggressive impulses, apparently untroubled by any feeling of guilt but unconsciously identified with his or her sadism.

2) A sense of the uncanny is experienced by obsessional neurotics when they feel they can 'work miracles' proving the omnipotence of their thoughts.

3) A sense of the uncanny may be experienced when other people fail to display some typical affective reaction which we should 'normally' expect to see in them, especially as a lack of fear betraying their omnipotent wishes.

4) A sense of the uncanny is experienced when we realise that we stand for another person or power in the relation of object and not, as we fondly imagined, of subject, especially of being lived by one's unconscious.

5) A sense of the uncanny is experienced when we witness the sudden and unexpected downfall of someone in power, meaning that as one identifies with the fallen person, the feeling of omnipotence is aroused.

6) Manifestations of unconscious psychic institutions – the id and the super-ego – arouse a sense of the uncanny. We

may distinguish three such manifestations: a) the compulsion to confess and the desire for punishment; b) the repetition-compulsion; c) repressed instinctual desires.

7) A sense of the uncanny is produced by certain forms of cynicism that appear free of guilt but are born from it.

8) A sense of the uncanny is produced when the subject's own omnipotence is projected onto others; figures of devil or demons.

9) A sense of the uncanny is produced by impenetrable silence on the part of another person; this arouses death-wishes and castration anxiety.

10) A sense of the uncanny is produced by something ineluctable. The most telling example of this type of uncanny feeling is that experienced by anyone who knows that the death of another is imminent. On account of unconscious feelings of omnipotence the person who has this knowledge feels as if at the same time he were the author of the death sentence.

11) A sense of the uncanny may accompany the sense of time or the feeling of 'infinity'; attempt to go beyond the life–death boundary.

12) A sense of the uncanny may be experienced when that which was begun in play passes into deadly earnest.

13) A sense of the uncanny is experienced by a particular group of masochists who must retain a masochistic solution to castration by orchestrating it in reality again and again.

All the examples seem to be moments that hinge on a question of power, mixed with life and death, with an overturning of norms. The main question seems to be: *Who is castrated? Who is the object of whom?* Bergler's concept of unconscious masochism and the uncanny is mentioned by both Jean Laplanche and Gilles Deleuze, and seems important in relation to the uncanny in so far as masochism is likewise an attempt to control castration anxiety.

Returning to my patient, a problem around omnipotence was immediately apparent in the exchange between us.

I was put in the position of saying something 'omnipotent' if I was the representative of these symptoms as psychological and not biological: was I saying I knew this, for a fact? Was I saying that she was doing this to herself (an idea which offended her immensely)? Was I saying something in her was capable of this much power to disrupt the physical and mental plane? The unconscious – what even is that? If I got close in any way to these co-ordinates, she would start rolling her eyes, becoming hostile, or question me about my beliefs. Fair enough, but it had a strange impact on me as I didn't feel I was trying to take up any position necessarily, and kept being lured into them, making it a chronic imminent threat. I've never had to care less.

I remember one moment in particular where I asked if she had any experiences of feeling out of place, or suddenly feeling confused about her position in the world. She inquired, 'What do you have in mind?' I said, these things happen sometimes, like during puberty, or moving towns, or going to college, and the co-ordinates change in us in some unexpected way. She was livid that I would be 'suggesting' that what she was experiencing could be the equivalent of a kid going to college. I replied that I wasn't suggesting any such equivalence, also that sometimes these experiences could be quite dire, but in any case, I was just wondering about different moments in her life. I didn't expect her to come back, she seemed so angry, but she did, and the next session she told me that for much of her childhood she believed that her family wasn't her real family. Also, that later in life she had discovered some information about her extended family and completely disowned them.

The question of this family that wasn't her family was present in her symptoms in so far as everything that she was experiencing was described as unfamiliar, or even a defamiliarisation of the familiar. She spoke of the feeling of presences, of hearing the sounds of voices, but also of not knowing where she was, of suddenly not recognising people.

While this might sound like a near-literal translation, classical hysterical-symptom speak, the difference was that saying it as she did was concrete – she didn't like the act of linking representations, which a hysteric takes to quite readily, or rather the symptom itself seems to do so in session. What was happening was a complete bifurcation and speaking about the symptoms seemed to give them more power, more autonomy.

I asked if these kinds of uncanny experiences had ever happened before the time period in question (basically the last two years), and at first she said no, with great resistance, but then alluded to an earlier experience of the feeling of a presence (seven years prior), that didn't scare her in the slightest in the way they now did. Why? She said at that moment it was without question what it was. I said, 'You mean a ghost?' She said yes. And now? 'I don't know what they are, they don't feel comforting in the way that felt at that moment.' One has to imagine it was comforting as a reassurance of immortality bringing to mind Freud's comment: 'Such ideas have sprung from the soil of unbounded self-love, from the primary narcissism which dominates the mind of the child and of primitive man. But when this stage has been surmounted, the double reverses its aspect. From having been an assurance of immortality, it becomes the uncanny harbinger of death.'[2] So here we have uncanny symptom time one – reassurance of immortality; and uncanny symptom time two – harbinger of death. This timeline is incredibly important.

I asked more about the difference between then and now, and she said she didn't know, but now the feeling was accompanied by so many other issues that just seemed bizarre to her, including hallucinations that weren't scary per se but were horrifying in so far as they were aesthetically displeasing to her, like exactly what she wouldn't pick to be afraid of. 'Like what?' I asked. 'I don't know, like stupid clowns and other horror movie images with bad colour schemes, not the kind of thing I like at all.' She said this with utmost feeling of revulsion,

even injustice, at the idea that she could be menaced by hallucinations so outside her aesthetic sensibilities. It is as if the
arousal of disgust added not only to the feeling of displeasure
and discomfort, but also to the feeling of its being foreign.

She then told the story of her earliest uncanny experience. She said she used to pray and that she loved to do
the rosary, though she claimed her family wasn't particularly
invested in religion, and the religious school she went to was
just the one that was there. She said she liked the rosary more
as a ritual than as an object of faith. So, one night she was
praying so hard that she was squeezing her eyes closed in the
act of prayer when she suddenly thought she saw something.
Maybe it was just the squeezing of her eyes, but . . . 'What
were you praying for?' I asked. 'Whatever, kid's things probably,' she answered, refusing to go any further. But why was she
praying so hard?

So much of this seems to speak to the abandoned or con-
quered infantile ideas, infantile omnipotent fantasies, early
modes of animism, belief in immortality, fears of divine castration, all of which were returning from the repressed. The
decathexis of these beliefs appeared not just in her symptoms,
but in her constant attitude of dismissal, no less the sheer
force of resistance that pervaded the dialogue with me, filled
with rationalisation and the attack on meaning or linking. It
was shocking to interact with; defences this pervasive often
feel characterological and not as if one is targeting discreet
phenomena, dealing with something hiding in plain sight.

There was a slipperiness in her relationship to language,
as if she wasn't anchored in it, which led to the extremes of
concreteness and abstractness at once, all of which had the
force of shattering speaking. Things needed to stay disjointed,
which itself added to the feeling of uncanniness, as if even I
was slipping from language and life, existing in an in-between
world. We might call the uncanny a representational attack on
representation, not unlike obsessionality, but different in so
far as the omnipotence isn't in the thought of the person, but

in their surroundings, handed over to reality. Reality is often what intrudes into an obsessional symptom picture; so what would intervene here?

I can't tell you how many times I just wanted to throw her out of the office. Was this her disavowed rage? Or is this just the reaction that one can have to this presence of the death drive undermining representation? What perhaps held me was the intense fascination exerted by the uncanny incidences themselves, especially with her symptoms, not least being the – to her, ugly – hallucinatory images, but also the actions that imposed themselves on her, from the idea of putting out a candle in her mouth, or opening the car door while the car was moving. The fascination and relief is probably having at the very least a manifest representation somewhere of the death drive itself, rather than this silent presence that was dragging us into the abyss.

The patient also experienced a kind of anxiety-signal which came as a feeling that she would go blind every time she was on a cross-walk – taking the form of 'in the next ten minutes you will go blind', which was a feeling more than it was a verbal thought. This chain of symptoms around seeing we were able to speak about together more readily, including a problem of seeing pictures of the most familiar others, like of Obama, and not recognising them, or forgetting a friend's identity to such a degree that she didn't even know if she knew who she was talking to, to waking up without any threads that could re-establish familiarity with where she was – just a blank. These difficulties in the scopophilic register were especially important since she worked as a photographer: it was her job to *see*, and she seemed to be in a process of being robbed of her eyes.

In fact, the question of her relationship to work was a turning point. She said, 'I do bad work.' This she didn't want questioned. 'It's just bad.' The harrowing thing being that she got away with it, that her industry just told itself that what was bad was good. She couldn't even convince people that it was bad. The firmness of this belief she wanted heard as real and rational, desiring a judgement and a punishment that never came, aside perhaps from her symptomatic decline. She wanted what was 'bad' to be revealed; she wanted punishment by *lex talionis*.

I asked in a session what bad meant to her. I said I found the word strange. She said, 'Bad is bad, what else could it mean?' I said that I thought it had a particularly moral, religious bent, like being a bad girl. She almost screamed, 'Is that what it means to *you*? Gross. I don't even want to know.' I said that I didn't think it was just me; that it must have a philological and historical backstory. She interrupted as if she couldn't stand to hear me speak. She went on to say that she *really* didn't like the idiosyncrasy of word usage and what it revealed about people. She did, however, look the word up before our next session and told me she was interested in the fact that 'bad' referred to a mannish woman, or to a hermaphrodite.

This moment gave me a sense of something important about her relationship to the symbolic world: not merely the disavowal of meaning or the ambivalence that disintegrated any hold on reality, but the horror of what language reveals about desire, about the specificity and idiosyncrasy of desire, which only appeared in her symptoms. What is uncanny, in fact, about language. 'Bad' felt like a pivot between this ghostly moralistic punitive uncanny universe and a whole field of sexual desire life which she did not speak about, or wasn't present in her speech itself.

Following this, after a session that she was very late for, she asked for an extra session. The end of this little vignette is going to be very banal; something that might be thought of also as a reverse feature of the uncanny. My patient came to the extra session to tell me that she had been seeing a woman she liked very much (she had vaguely alluded to her several times without going into it): she had appeared almost miraculously, and their relationship was time-limited, which was a blessing in disguise, because she couldn't make love to a woman whom she liked.

With this woman, they were doing their best to work it through, she had a good sense of humour about it, and was very patient. 'What happens?' I asked. '*You know*,' she said, with a strange certainty. Of course I had no idea what she was talking about. I looked at her quizzically. She said she didn't want to talk about it anymore right now, at least not in any detail, and we moved onto other things, including her father's morbid fear of dying, which had worsened significantly after watching *his* mother die slowly over the last six years.

Fast-forward three sessions. It turned out that when she was about to make love with this woman she almost blacked out, or maybe felt as if she was going to, it wasn't clear, but the perceptual field narrowed, something happened in her body, she could sometimes lose control, and even start to feel like she didn't know where she was. 'When did this first happen?' I asked. About three years ago was the first time. 'From before all the symptoms started?' I asked. Yes, she replied coolly and without any interest, at which point she told me an incredible story of uncanny repetition: every woman this had happened with, five to be exact, had the exact same characteristics, she admired them all intensely for the way they lived, contra her bad living; they were divorcing men; they were incredibly intelligent and funny and she felt them to be twins or doubles in their sensibilities (return of the reassuring double as ghost in the form of a love object). Once, she proffered, a psychic told her she would be with this woman. 'Who or which one?' I asked. 'A divorcée,' she said. 'Oh, that you steal from a man?' She screamed again. 'I guess it's hard to hear it out loud like that. Gross. Okay, I take it. Is it time to stop? I wish you had a clock in here.'

Isn't it incredible that no one had asked about her sex life in relation to her symptoms for the two years she was in a state of complete disintegration, or that she concealed the sexual origins of her symptom, even to herself? Sexual love reawakens a whole configuration of thoughts on mortality, omnipotence, castration, that can appear from the out-side-in, in the most radical fashion, with the most extreme forms of resistance.

Lacan, speaking about anxiety and its transformation in psy-choanalysis, provides a fascinating case, one of the few of his own that he spoke of in any detail. The case begins with the withdrawal of the patient's husband's excessive atten-tion which had sustained her, including a complaint about it. Lacan says she suddenly begins to speak with a peculiar preci-sion (as opposed to, for example, the vagueness of my patient) about her state. He writes:

> This woman . . . bears witness to what occurs for her if, when she is driving, for example, an alert flashes up for a moving entity that makes her say to herself something along the lines of *God, a car!* Well, inexplicably, she notices the existence of a vaginal swelling. This is what strikes her that day and she notes that, during some periods, the phenomenon will occur when just any old object comes into her visual field, to all appearances utterly foreign to anything of a sexual nature.[3]

Here we see that, rather than ending with the impossibility of sexual love, we begin with its sudden explosive manifesta-tion. Any object that enters the patients visual field isn't sco-tomised, but instead triggers an experience of *jouissance* that arises like a flash, a signal, as the other face of anxiety or the uncanny, transforming terror into an excited feeling in her body. This leads the patient to speak to the peculiarities of the nature of her analytic relationship to Lacan. He says about it: 'Each of her initiatives are dedicated to me, her analyst. *I can't say devoted,* she adds, *that would mean it was done with a certain aim, but no, any old object forces me to evoke you as a witness, not even to have your approval of what I see, no, simply your gaze, and*

in saying that, I'm going slightly too far, let's say that this gaze helps me to make each thing assume meaning.'⁴
What we see is that this exciting object is linked to the function of the gaze in the transference. This is not the demanding clumsy gaze of her husband, nor even her desirous looking (especially her looking for Lacan's approval), but something about the analyst as witness, the one who watches this emergence of desire in a field that surrounds her. This is the circuit that the other is used to support, not for judgement or even knowledge, but to allow each thing to assume meaning. She corrects herself, saying that it isn't any meaning in particular, but meaning as such. The world is suddenly an infinite meaningful field – without, for all that, taking on any particular narrative. Think about this in contrast to the shredding of meaning and the characteristics of denial of my patient, but also the excessive meaning with respect to omnipotent fantasies in uncanny clinical phenomena concerning, power, life and death.

Lacan's patient goes on to speak about the phenomena of falling in love. She says about her first love that she enveloped herself in a series of lies like a cocoon in order to be exactly what she wanted to be in her lover's eyes. With Lacan, there is a difference. He writes: 'After all, what she wanted was not so much for me to look at her as for my gaze to replace hers. *"I appeal to the assistance of your person. The gaze, my gaze, is insufficient when it comes to capturing everything that stands to be absorbed from the outside. It's not about watching me do something, it's about doing it for me."'⁵*

I find this statement about what transference can do absolutely beautiful: the idea of an appeal for assistance in order to capture the everything that can be taken in from the outside; the insufficiency of one when it comes to the desire for this absorption; and the necessity that this extend beyond mere meaning. She is not taking the other in, duping them, nor is she taken in by her own ideal; rather, she allows her gaze to drop by replacing it with her analyst's eyes, almost feels him to be doing the looking. It is through this falling away of her gaze that the world flares up.

Could we not imagine that in some way this 'fall of gaze' is what my patient was seeking in her psychogenic blindness, her blackouts, her declaration of herself as bad, and even her aesthetically displeasing hallucinations (really indexing the image as looked at)?

What Lacan is showing is that the transference is not the establishment of reciprocity but the possibility that arises from the achievement of real separation. This allows the object to act as a supplement and not as a negative, anxiety-inducing, uncanny cipher. Lacan writes, 'If what is most me lies on the outside, not because I *projected* it there but because it was cut off from me, the paths I shall take to retrieve it can afford an altogether different variety.'[6]

Between Lacan and his patient, a strange functionality arises, like two bodies humming, a woman without eyes, an analyst without a body, and an object given all the life there is to give it. The gaze dropped, she finds an infinite possibility in the world around her, born by the insufficiency, as she says, of one in the face of so much; this new vision of reality that she has fallen in love with and finds herself wanting, all of it. Conversion here isn't in the direction of the uncanny, but transforms the uncanny, bringing it into the field of desire. I hope this is where my patient and I will find ourselves, soon.

My Country 'Tis

There is a clinical case of Selma Fraiberg's, discussed in her 1972 article 'Some Characteristics of Genital Arousal and Discharge in Latency Girls'.[1] Fraiberg investigates genital arousal in pre-pubescent girls, awareness of the vagina, early experiences of vaginal orgasm and states of genital anaesthesia in children and adult analysands. She goes a long way to re-centralising castration anxiety, not in relation to 'not having a penis', as it were, nor clitoral substitutes or deepened female masochism, but with a particular kind of turning away from peaks of excitement and experiences of pleasure that feel unending.

Fraiberg speaks of failed attempts to undergird this excitement through the elaboration of fantasies or 'stories' because they induce guilt, bring the little girl too close, on the one hand, to experiences of the omnipotence of the mother, and, on the other hand, dread of penetration by the father. The search for this lost pleasure, is what she then hears repeated in her adult female patients.

Fraiberg asks a little girl she names Nancy to explain to her the feelings that she says 'don't get finished' and frighten her. She says, 'You know what it's like? It's like when you're playing the piano. Suppose you play *do, re, me,* and *fa.* Well, the *fa* is like just crying for *sol* to get finished. It's like a baby whining for its mother.' Do the feelings ever get finished, Fraiberg asks her again. Well, no, says Nancy – seemingly annoyed that Fraiberg has failed to comment on the extraordinary articulation she gives to the problem at hand. She then launches into an explanation of what it's like:

'All right. It went like this. [She now sang in a queer atonal voice, using, of all things, the first phrase of "My country, 'tis of thee".] All right it goes like this. *My country 'tis . . . my country 'tis . . . my country 'tis . . .*'

She seemed prepared to repeat this interminably.

Finally, I asked: 'And how does it get finished?'

Nancy: 'Well, it ends when I go to sleep.'[2]

Acknowledgements

My publishers and editors, Eleanor Ivory Weber and Camilla Wills, and myself have W surnames, like a wolf pack: Weber, Webster, Wills. This book only exists thanks to their vision, their belief in me, and their work of weaving these texts together. Having the chance to hear about their encounter with my work, their desire to gather these revelations together into a book that spoke across disciplines, was a rare exchange. No one likes cleaning out the closet; doing so with them – revisiting parts of myself that I've mistakenly wanted to forget – was difficult and humbling. I think this intimacy is present in the book you hold in your hands, which was also conceived during the time that I was pregnant, gave birth to my daughter, and during the first six months of her life. Camilla will also have given birth by the time this book goes to print. My gratitude to both of them, and to Jacob Blandy for his eagle-eye copyediting.

For giving me time and space, I thank my daughter and her father: Alma Anne Brown and Richard Brown. Both of you are my disorganising force of desire.

'The Disorganising Force of Desire' is a version of an essay – 'On the Question of the Future of Psychoanalysis: Some Reflections on Jacques Lacan' – previously published in the *European Journal of Psychoanalysis* (2014). A version of 'Dream Life' was published as 'Dreaming in Exile or the Exile of Dreams' in *Constellations* 23, no. 2 (June 2016). A longer version of 'Variations on a Standard' was published in *Reading Lacan's* Écrits: *From 'Logical Time' to 'Response to Jean Hyppolite'*, edited by Derek Hook, Calum Neill and

Stijn Vanheule (Routledge, 2022). 'Death Drive' was previously published as 'The Death Drive: Hypothesis or Clinical Guarantee' in *Research in Psychoanalysis* 2, no. 26 (December 2018). 'Masturbation Fantasies' was previously published in *Apology Magazine* 5 (autumn 2019). 'Male Sexuality and Genitality' was published in issue A10 of the magazine *Richardson* (2021), and forms part of a longer piece written with Marcus Coelen on Sándor Ferenczi and genital sexuality, forthcoming in *Psychoanalysis, Gender and Sexualities: From Feminism to Trans**, edited by Patricia Gherovici and Manya Steinkoler (Routledge, 2022). A version of 'A Young Boy and His Mother' was published in *Lacan, Psychoanalysis, and Comedy*, edited by Patricia Gherovici (Cambridge University Press, 2016). A version of 'On the Ongoing Realities of Sexual Abuse' was published as 'Let Cold Fires Burn' in *Penumbr(a): A Journal of Psychoanalysis & Modernity* 1 (2021). Some of the work in 'Useless Organs' comes from a previous article entitled '*Memento Mori*: The Book as a Cut', published in *Studies in Gender and Sexuality* 17, no. 1 (2016). 'Sex Panic' was previously published as 'Panic' in *SSENSE Magazine* (2019). A version of 'Uncanny Sexualities' was published as 'Uncanny Conversions' in *RISS Materialien* 6 (Textem, 2020).

Notes

The following abbreviation is used in the notes and bibliography:

SE *The Standard Edition of the Complete Psychological Works of Sigmund Freud*, trans. James Strachey in collaboration with Anna Freud, assisted by Alix Strachey and Alan Tyson, 24 vols (London: Hogarth Press, 1966–74).

The Disorganising Force of Desire

1. See Sigmund Freud, *The Future of an Illusion* (1927), in *SE* XXI.
2. Sigmund Freud, *Civilization and Its Discontents* (1930), in *SE* XXI, 144–5.
3. Jacques Lacan, *My Teaching*, trans. David Macey (London: Verso, 2008), 95.
4. Ibid., 105.
5. See Jacques Lacan, *The Seminar of Jacques Lacan, Book VII: The Ethics of Psychoanalysis, 1959–1960*, ed. Jacques-Alain Miller, trans. Dennis Porter (New York: W.W. Norton, 1997).
6. Philip Rieff, *Freud: The Mind of a Moralist* (Chicago, IL: University of Chicago Press, 1979).
7. Sigmund Freud, *Three Essays on the Theory of Sexuality* (1905), in *SE* VII.
8. Sigmund Freud, 'The Future Prospects of Psycho-Analytic Therapy' (1910), in *SE* XI, 141.
9. Ibid.
10. Ibid., 146.
11. Ibid.
12. Ibid., 147.
13. Ibid.
14. Ibid., 148.
15. Ibid., 150–51.
16. See Jacques Lacan, *Feminine Sexuality: Jacques Lacan and the École Freudienne*, ed. Juliet Mitchell and Jacqueline Rose, trans. Jacqueline Rose (New York: W.W. Norton, 1982); Lisa Appignanesi and John Forrester, *Freud's Women* (New York: Other Press, 2001); and Paul Verhaeghe, *Does the Woman Exist? From Freud's Hysteric to Lacan's Feminine*, trans. Marc Du Ry (London: Rebus Press, 1999).
17. See Lacan, *Feminine Sexuality*; Nancy J. Chodorow, *Feminism and Psychoanalytic Theory* (New Haven, CT: Yale University Press, 1991); Walter Benjamin, *Illuminations*, ed. Hannah Arendt, trans. Harry Zohn (New York: Schocken, 2007); Judith Butler, *Gender Trouble: Feminism and the Subversion of Identity* (London: Routledge, 1990).

18. Erik Homburger Erikson, 'The Dream Specimen of Psychoanalysis', *Journal of the American Psychoanalytic Association* 2, no. 1 (January 1954).
19. Sigmund Freud, *The Interpretation of Dreams* (1900), *SE* IV, 116–17.
20. Erikson, 'Dream Specimen', 45.
21. Ibid., 45–6.
22. Freud to Karl Abraham, 9 January 1908, in Ernst Falzeder, ed., *The Complete Correspondence of Sigmund Freud and Karl Abraham, 1907–1925*, trans. Caroline Schwarzacher with the collaboration of Christine Trollope and Klara Majthenyi King (London: Karnac, 2002), 21.
23. Appignanesi and Forrester, *Freud's Women*, 127.
24. Freud, *Interpretation of Dreams*, *SE* IV, 112.
25. See Jacques Lacan, 'The Mirror Stage as Formative of the *I* Function as Revealed in Psychoanalytic Experience', in Lacan, *Écrits: The First Complete Edition in English*, trans. Bruce Fink (New York: W.W. Norton, 2006).
26. Freud, *Interpretation of Dreams*, *SE* IV, 483.
27. Jacques Lacan, *The Seminar of Jacques Lacan, Book XVII: The Other Side of Psychoanalysis*, trans. Russell Grigg (New York: W.W. Norton, 2007).
28. Serge Leclaire, *Psychoanalyzing: On the Order of the Unconscious and the Practice of the Letter*, trans. Peggy Kamuf (Stanford, CA: Stanford University Press, 1998), 36–7.
29. Ibid., 32–3.
30. Ibid., 33.
31. Ibid.
32. Sigmund Freud, 'Lines of Advance in Psycho-Analytic Therapy' (1919), in *SE* XVII, 157.
33. Ibid.
34. Ibid., 164–5.
35. Ibid.
36. Ibid., 163.
37. Terry Eagleton, *Reason, Faith, and Revolution: Reflections on the God Debate* (New Haven, CT: Yale University Press, 2009), 89–90.
38. Adorno quoted in ibid., 91.

Dream Life

1. For a history of French psychoanalysis see Élisabeth Roudinesco, *Jacques Lacan & Co.: A History of Psychoanalysis in France, 1925–1985*, trans. Jeffrey Mehlman (Chicago, IL: University of Chicago Press, 1989).
2. See Jacques Lacan, 'The Direction of the Treatment and the Principles of Its Power', in Lacan, *Écrits*.
3. Theodor W. Adorno, *Dream Notes*, ed. Henri Lonitz and Christoph Gödde, trans. Rodney Livingstone (Cambridge: Polity Press, 2007).
4. Ibid., vi.
5. Theodor W. Adorno, *The Culture Industry: Selected Essays on Mass Culture*, ed. J.M. Bernstein (New York: Routledge, 2001).
6. Adorno, *Dream Notes*, 54.
7. Ibid.

8. Theodor W. Adorno, 'Opinion Delusion Society', in Adorno, *Critical Models: Interventions and Catchwords*, trans. Henry W. Pickford (New York: Columbia University Press, 1998), 120.

9. Adorno, *Dream Notes*, 14–15.

10. See Sigmund Freud, 'Lecture XXXII: Anxiety and Instinctual Life' (1933), in *SE* XVI, and Lacan, *Seminar: The Other Side of Psychoanalysis*.

11. Sigmund Freud, 'Mourning and Melancholia' (1917), in *SE* XIV, 249.

12. Adorno, *Dream Notes*, 75.

13. Jan Philipp Reemtsma, 'Afterword', in ibid., 92–3.

14. Ibid., 63–4.

15. Theodor W. Adorno, *Aesthetic Theory*, ed. and trans. Robert Hullot-Kentor (New York: Continuum, 2002), 74.

16. Jacques Lacan, *The Seminar of Jacques Lacan, Book II: The Ego in Freud's Theory and in the Technique of Psychoanalysis, 1954–1955*, ed. Jacques-Alain Miller, trans. Sylvana Tomaselli (Cambridge: Cambridge Univerity Press, 1988), 171.

17. Adorno, *Dream Notes*, 94.

Action in Analysis

1. Lacan's Seminar XV has not to date been published in book form in an English translation; Cormac Gallagher's translation can be found online.

2. Hans W. Loewald, 'On the Therapeutic Action of Psychoanalysis', in Loewald, *The Work of Hans Loewald: An Introduction and Commentary*, ed. Gerald I. Fogel (Lanham, MD: Jason Aronson, 1991).

3. Ibid., 30.

End Your Analysis!

1. See Sigmund Freud, 'Analysis of a Phobia in a Five-Year-Old Boy' (1909), in *SE* X.

2. See Sigmund Freud, 'Fragment of an Analysis of a Case of Hysteria' (1905), in *SE* VII.

3. Jane Gallop, 'Keys to Dora', in *In Dora's Case: Freud, Hysteria, Feminism*, ed. Charles Bernheimer and Claire Kahan (London: Virago, 1985), 215.

4. Freud, 'Fragment of an Analysis of a Case of Hysteria', 109.

5. See Sigmund Freud, 'Notes upon a Case of Obsessional Neurosis' (1909), in *SE* X.

6. See Sigmund Freud, 'Psycho-Analytic Notes on an Autobiographical Account of a Case of Paranoia (*Dementia Paranoides*)' (1911), in *SE* XII.

7. See Sigmund Freud, 'From the History of an Infantile Neurosis' (1918), in *SE* XVII.

Variations on a Standard

1. Jacques Lacan, 'Variations on the Standard Treatment', in Lacan, *Écrits*.
2. Jacques Lacan, 'The Direction of the Treatment and the Principles of Its Power', in Lacan, *Écrits*, 489–542.
3. Lacan, *Variations on the Standard Treatment*, 327.
4. Ibid., 324.
5. Sigmund Freud, 'Observations on Transference-Love (Further Recommendations on the Technique of Psycho-Analysis III)' (1915), in *SE* XII, 171; Lacan, *Variations on the Standard Treatment*, 324.
6. Ibid., 325.
7. Ibid.
8. Ibid.
9. Ibid., 325–36.
10. Edward Glover, 'Therapeutic Criteria of Psycho-Analysis', *International Journal of Psychoanalysis* 35 (1954): 96; my italics.
11. Ibid.
12. Lacan, 'Variations on the Standard Treatment', 327.
13. Glover, 'Therapeutic Criteria', 99.
14. Ibid., 99–100.
15. Lacan, 'Variations on the Standard Treatment', 329.
16. Ibid., 330.
17. Ibid.
18. Ibid.
19. Ibid.
20. Ibid., 330–31.
21. Ibid., 331.
22. Ibid.
23. Ibid.
24. Ibid.
25. Ibid., 331–2.
26. Ibid., 332.
27. Ibid., 332–5.
28. Ibid., 332.
29. Ibid.
30. See Sigmund Freud, 'Project for a Scientific Psychology' (1950), in *SE* I, and Freud and Josef Breuer, *Studies on Hysteria* (1893–95), in *SE* II.
31. See Jacques Lacan, 'Aggressivity in Psychoanalysis', in Lacan, *Écrits*.
32. Peter Fonagy and Mary Target, 'Playing with the Reality of Analytic Love: Commentary on Paper by Jody Messler Davies "Falling in Love with Love"', *Psychoanalytic Dialogues* 14, no. 4 (2004).
33. Lacan, 'Variations on the Standard Treatment', 339.
34. Ibid.
35. Ibid., 340.
36. Ibid., 340–41.
37. Ferenczi to Freud, 25 October 1925, in Ernst Falzeder and Eva Brabant with Patrizia Giampieri-Deutsch, eds, *The Correspondence of Sigmund Freud and Sándor Ferenczi*, Volume 3: 1919–1933, trans. Peter T. Hoffer (Cambridge:

Cambridge University Press, 2000), 233–4.

38. Lacan, 'Variations on the Standard Treatment', 341.
39. Ibid.
40. Wilhelm Reich, *Character Analysis*, trans. Vincent R. Carfagno (New York: Farrar, Straus and Giroux, 1980).
41. Lacan, 'Variations on the Standard Treatment', 342.
42. Ibid.
43. Ibid., 343.
44. Ibid.
45. Ibid.
46. Ibid.
47. Ibid., 344.
48. Ibid., 344–5.
49. Ibid., 345.
50. Ibid.
51. Ibid., 346.
52. Ibid., 346–7.
53. Ibid., 348–9.
54. Ibid., 347.
55. Ibid.
56. Ibid., 349.
57. Ibid., 350.
58. Ibid.
59. Ibid.
60. Lacan's Seminar XIV has not to date been published in book form in an English translation; Cormac Gallagher's translation can be found online.
61. Lacan, *Variations on the Standard Treatment*, 350–51.
62. Ibid., 351.
63. Ibid., 353.
64. Ibid., 353–4.
65. Ibid., 354.
66. Ibid., 353–4.
67. Ibid., 354.
68. Ibid.
69. Ibid., 354–5.
70. Ibid., 355.
71. Ibid., 357.
72. Ibid., 358.
73. Ibid.
74. Ibid.
75. Ibid.
76. Ibid.
77. Maxwell Gitelson, 'Therapeutic Problems in the Analysis of the "Normal" Candidate', *International Journal of Psychoanalysis* 35 (1954).
78. Lacan, 'Variations on the Standard Treatment', 359.
79. Ibid.
80. Ibid., 360.
81. Ibid.

82. Ibid.
83. Ibid.
84. Sigmund Freud, 'Recommendations to Physicians Practising Psycho-Analysis' (1912), in *SE* XII, 120.

Death Drive

1. Sigmund Freud, 'The Subtleties of a Faulty Action' (1935), in *SE* XXII, 235.
2. Ibid., 233.
3. Ibid., 234.
4. Ibid.
5. Sigmund Freud, 'A Disturbance of Memory on the Acropolis' (1936), in *SE* XXII.
6. See Lacan, *Seminar: The Ethics of Psychoanalysis*.
7. Jacques Lacan, *The Seminar of Jacques Lacan, Book XX: On Feminine Sexuality, the Limits of Love and Knowledge, Encore 1972–1973*, ed. Jacques-Alain Miller, trans. Bruce Fink (New York: W.W. Norton, 1999), 47.

Loneliness

1. Rosine Lefort, in collaboration with Robert Lefort, *Birth of the Other*, trans. Marc Du Ry, Lindsay Watson and Leonardo Rodríguez (Chicago: University of Illinois Press, 1994), 17.
2. Ibid., 3–6.
3. Ibid., 37.
4. Ibid., 7–8.
5. Ibid.
6. Ibid., xvii.
7. Ibid., 167–90.
8. See Lacan's Seminar XXIII, 'The Sinthome or Joyce and the Sinthome' (1975–1976), not to date published in book form in an English translation; Cormac Gallagher's translation can be found online.
9. Lefort, *Birth of the Other*, 110.
10. See Melanie Klein, 'On the Sense of Loneliness (1963)', in Klein, *Envy and Gratitude and Other Works, 1946–1963* (New York: Free Press, 1984).
11. Lefort, *Birth of the Other*, 211–13.

There Is No Common Satisfaction

1. Freud to Fliess, 23 August 1894, in Jeffrey Moussaieff Masson, ed. and trans., *The Complete Letters of Sigmund Freud to Wilhelm Fliess* (Cambridge, MA: Harvard University Press, 1985), 91–5.
2. Jacques Lacan, *The Seminar of Jacques Lacan, Book X: Anxiety*, ed. Jacques-Alain Miller, trans. Adrian Price (Cambridge: Polity, 2014), 247.

Masturbation Fantasies

1. Sigmund Freud, '"A Child Is Being Beaten": A Contribution to the Study of the Origin of Sexual Perversions', in *SE* XVII, 193.
2. Ibid., 179–81.
3. Ibid., 187–8.
4. Ibid., 185–6.

Male Sexuality and Genitality

1. Sándor Ferenczi, *Thalassa: A Theory of Genitality*, trans. Henry Alden Bunker (London: Karnac, 1989), 56.
2. See Sigmund Freud, *A Phylogenetic Fantasy: Overview of the Transference Neurosis*, ed. Ilse Grubrich-Simitis and trans. Axel Hoffer and Peter T. Hoffer (Cambridge, MA and London: Belknap Press, 1987).
3. Ferenczi, *Thalassa*, 50.
4. Ibid., 43.
5. Ferenczi to Freud, 13 May 1914, in Eva Brabant, Ernst Falzeder and Patrizia Giampieri-Deutsch, eds, *The Correspondence of Sigmund Freud and Sándor Ferenczi: Volume 1, 1908–1914*, trans. Peter T. Hoffer (Cambridge: Cambridge University Press, 1993), 553–4.
6. Sándor Ferenczi, *The Clinical Diary of Sándor Ferenczi*, ed. Judith Dupont, trans. Michael Balint and Nicola Zarday Jackson (Cambridge, MA: Harvard University Press, 1995), 187.
7. Ibid.
8. Freud to Ferenczi, 16 September 1930, and Ferenczi to Freud, 21 September 1930, in Falzeder, Brabant and Giampieri-Deutsch, eds, *The Correspondence of Sigmund Freud and Sándor Ferenczi, Volume 3: 1919–1933*, 399–401.

A Young Boy and His Mother

1. See Sigmund Freud, *Jokes and Their Relation to the Unconscious* (1905), *SE* VIII and 'Humour' (1927), in *SE* XXI, 159–66.
2. See Jacques Lacan, *The Seminar of Jacques Lacan, Book XI: The Four Fundamental Concepts of Psychoanalysis*, ed. Jacques-Alain Miller, trans. Alan Sheridan (New York: W.W. Norton, 1998).

Dream

1. Nathanael West, *Miss Lonelyhearts* (New York: New Directions, n.d. [1946]), 1.
2. Ibid., 20–21.

On the Ongoing Realities of Sexual Abuse

1. See Freud and Breuer, *Studies on Hysteria*.
2. See ibid.
3. Sigmund Freud, 'Constructions in Analysis' (1937), in *SE* XXIII, 267–8.
4. See Sigmund Freud, *Totem and Taboo* (1912–13), in *SE* XIII; '"Civilized" Sexual Morality and Modern Nervous Illness' (1908), in *SE* IX; *Three Essays on the Theory of Sexuality*; 'The Taboo of Virginity (Contributions to the Psychology of Love III)' (1918), in SE XI; *Civilization and Its Discontents*.
5. See Freud to Fliess, 6 December 1896, in Masson, ed., *Complete Letters of Sigmund Freud to Wilhelm Fliess*, 207–15; Freud and Breuer, *Studies on Hysteria*; and Freud, 'Constructions in Analysis'.
6. See Sigmund Freud, 'The Neuro-Psychoses of Defence' (1894), in *SE* III, and 'Inhibitions, Symptoms and Anxiety' (1926), in *SE* XX.
7. Jacques Lacan, *The Seminar of Jacques Lacan, Book III: The Psychoses, 1955–1956*, ed. Jacques-Alain Miller, trans. Russell Grigg (New York: W.W. Norton, 1997), 19.
8. Ibid., 21.
9. Ibid.
10. Ibid., 39.
11. Ibid., 245.
12. See Freud, 'Psycho-Analytic Notes on an Autobiographical Account of a Case of Paranoia'.
13. Lacan, *Seminar: The Psychoses*, 90.
14. Freud, 'Mourning and Melancholia', 249.
15. Lacan, *Seminar: The Psychoses*, 91.
16. Ibid.
17. Ibid.
18. Ibid., 178.

Useless Organs

1. Paul B Preciado, *Can the Monster Speak? Report to an Academy of Psychoanalysts*, trans. Frank Wynne (Pasadena, CA: Semiotext(e), 2020), 98.
2. Paul B. Preciado, *Testo Junkie: Sex, Drugs, and Biopolitics in the Pharmacopornographic Era*, trans. Bruce Benderson (New York: Feminist Press, 2013); Jamieson Webster, *Conversion Disorder: Listening to the Body in Psychoanalysis* (New York: Columbia University Press, 2018).
3. Preciado, *Testo Junkie*, 359.
4. Ibid., 359–60.
5. Paul B. Preciado, *An Apartment on Uranus: Chronicles of the Crossing*, trans. Charlotte Mandell (Pasadena, CA: Semiotext(e), 2019), 204–5.
6. Jamieson Webster, Alison Gingeras and Paul B. Preciado, 'Pathologically Optimistic: An Interview with Paul Preciado', *Gagosian Quarterly* (winter 2020), https://gagosian.com/quarterly/2020/12/04/interview-pathologically-optimistic-paul-b-preciado/.
7. Ibid.

8. Sigmund Freud, 'Draft M. The Architecture of Hysteria, May 25, 1897', in Masson, ed., *Complete Letters of Sigmund Freud to Wilhelm Fliess*, 246–8.
9. Preciado, *Testo Junkie*, 389.
10. Ibid., 400–401.
11. Freud, 'Observations on Transference-Love', 171.
12. Freud and Breuer, *Studies on Hysteria*, 297.

Sex Panic

1. Sigmund Freud, *Beyond the Pleasure Principle* (1920), in *SE* XVIII, 56–7.
2. Melanie Klein, 'Some Theoretical Conclusions Regarding the Emotional Life of the Infant', in Klein, *Envy and Gratitude and Other Works, 1946–1963* (New York: Free Press, 1984).

Uncanny Sexualities

1. Edmund Bergler, 'The Psycho-Analysis of the Uncanny', *International Journal of Psychoanalysis* 15 (1934): 221; italics in original.
2. Sigmund Freud, 'The "Uncanny"' (1919), in *SE* XVII, 235.
3. Lacan, *Seminar: Anxiety*, 188.
4. Ibid.
5. Ibid., 189.
6. Ibid., 223.

My Country 'Tis

1. Selma Fraiberg, 'Some Characteristics of Genital Arousal and Discharge in Latency Girls', *Pschoanalytic Study of the Child* 27 (1972).
2. Ibid., 452–3.

Bibliography

Adorno, Theodor W. *Negative Dialectics.* Translated by E.B. Ashton. New York: Continuum, 1973.
—— 'Opinion Delusion Society'. In Theodor W. Adorno, *Critical Models: Interventions and Catchwords*, 105–22. Translated by Henry W. Pickford. New York: Columbia University Press, 1998.
—— *The Culture Industry: Selected Essays on Mass Culture.* Edited by J.M. Bernstein. New York: Routledge, 2001.
—— *Aesthetic Theory.* Edited and translated by Robert Hullot-Kentor. New York: Continuum, 2002.
—— *Dream Notes.* Edited by Henri Lonitz and Christoph Gödde, translated by Rodney Livingstone. Cambridge: Polity Press, 2007.
Adorno, Theodor W. and Max Horkheimer. *Dialectic of Enlightenment: Philosophical Fragments.* Translated by Edmund Jephcott. Stanford, CA: Stanford University Press, 2002.
Appignanesi, Lisa and John Forrester. *Freud's Women.* New York: Other Press, 2001.
Benjamin, Walter. *Illuminations.* Edited by Hannah Arendt, translated by Harry Zohn. New York: Schocken, 2007.
Bergler, Edmund. 'The Psycho-Analysis of the Uncanny'. *International Journal of Psychoanalysis* 15 (1934): 215–44.
Brabant, Eva, Ernst Falzeder and Patrizia Giampieri-Deutsch, eds. *The Correspondence of Sigmund Freud and Sándor Ferenczi: Volume 1, 1908-1914.* Translated by Peter T. Hoffer. Cambridge: Cambridge University Press, 1993.
Butler, Judith. *Gender Trouble: Feminism and the Subversion of Identity.* London: Routledge, 1990.
Chodorow, Nancy J. *Feminism and Psychoanalytic Theory.* New Haven, CT: Yale University Press, 1991
Erikson, Erik Homburger. 'The Dream Specimen Of Psychoanalysis'. *Journal of the American Psychoanalytic Association* 2, no. 1 (January 1954): 5–56.
Falzeder, Ernst, ed. *The Complete Correspondence of Sigmund Freud and Karl Abraham, 1907-1925.* Translated by Caroline Schwarzacher with the collaboration of Christine Trollope and Klara Majthenyi King. London: Karnac, 2002.
Falzeder, Ernst and Eva Brabant with Patrizia Giampieri-Deutsch, eds. *The Correspondence of Sigmund Freud and Sándor Ferenczi, Volume 3: 1919-1933.* Translated by Peter T. Hoffer. Cambridge: Cambridge University Press, 2000.
Ferenczi, Sándor. *Thalassa: A Theory of Genitality.* Translated by Henry Alden Bunker. London: Karnac, 1989.
—— *The Clinical Diary of Sándor Ferenczi.* Edited by Judith Dupont, translated

by Michael Balint and Nicola Zarday Jackson. Cambridge, MA: Harvard University Press, 1995.

Fonagy, Peter and Mary Target. 'Playing with the Reality of Analytic Love: Commentary on Paper by Jody Messler Davies "Falling in Love with Love". *Psychoanalytic Dialogues* 14, no. 4 (2004): 503–15.

Fraiberg, Selma. 'Some Characteristics of Genital Arousal and Discharge in Latency Girls'. *Pschoanalytic Study of the Child* 27 (1972): 439–75.

Freud, Sigmund. 'The Neuro-Psychoses of Defence' (1894). In *SE* III, 43–61.

——— *The Interpretation of Dreams* (1900). *SE* IV.

——— 'Fragment of an Analysis of a Case of Hysteria' (1905). In *SE* VII, 1–122.

——— *Jokes and Their Relation to the Unconscious* (1905). *SE* VIII.

——— *Three Essays on the Theory of Sexuality* (1905). In *SE* VII, 155–243.

——— '"Civilized" Sexual Morality and Modern Nervous Illness' (1908). In *SE* IX, 177–204.

——— 'Analysis of a Phobia in a Five-Year-Old Boy' (1909). In *SE* X, 1–150.

——— 'Notes upon a Case of Obsessional Neurosis' (1909). In *SE* X, 151–318.

——— 'The Future Prospects of Psycho-Analytic Therapy' (1910). In *SE* XI, 139–52.

——— 'Psycho-Analytic Notes on an Autobiographical Account of a Case of Paranoia' (1911). In *SE* XII, 1–82.

——— 'Recommendations to Physicians Practising Psycho-Analysis' (1912). In *SE* XII, 109–20.

——— *Totem and Taboo* (1912–13). In *SE* XIII, 1–162.

——— 'Observations on Transference-Love (Further Recommendations on the Technique of Psycho-Analysis III)' (1915). In *SE* XII, 157–71.

——— 'Mourning and Melancholia' (1917). In *SE* XIV, 237–58.

——— 'From the History of an Infantile Neurosis' (1918). In *SE* XVII, 1–122.

——— 'The Taboo of Virginity (Contributions to the Psychology of Love III)' (1918). In *SE* XI, 191–208.

——— '"A Child Is Being Beaten": A Contribution to the Study of the Origin of Sexual Perversions' (1919). In *SE* XVII, 175–204.

——— 'Lines of Advance in Psycho-Analytic Therapy' (1919). In *SE* XVII, 157–68.

——— 'The "Uncanny"' (1919). In *SE* XVII, 217–56.

——— *Beyond the Pleasure Principle* (1920). In *SE* XVIII, 1–64.

——— *Group Psychology and the Analysis of the Ego* (1921). In *SE* XVIII, 65–144.

——— 'Inhibitions, Symptoms and Anxiety' (1926). In *SE* XX, 75–176.

——— 'Humour' (1927). In *SE* XXI, 159–66.

——— *The Future of an Illusion* (1927). In *SE* XVII, 1–56.

——— *Civilization and Its Discontents* (1930). In *SE* XXI, 57–146.

——— 'Lecture XXXII: Anxiety and Instinctual Life' (1933). In *SE* XXII, 81–111.

——— 'The Subtleties of a Faulty Action' (1935). In *SE* XXII, 231–6.

——— 'A Disturbance of Memory on the Acropolis' (1936). In *SE* XXII, 237–48.

——— 'Analysis Terminable and Interminable' (1937). In *SE* XXIII, 209–54.

——— 'Constructions in Analysis' (1937). In *SE* XXIII, 255–70.

——— 'Project for a Scientific Psychology' (1950). In *SE* I, 283–387.

——— *A Phylogenetic Fantasy: Overview of the Transference Neurosis.* Edited by Ilse Grubrich-Simitis and translated by Axel Hoffer and Peter T. Hoffer. Cambridge, MA and London: Belknap Press, 1987.

Freud, Sigmund and Josef Breuer. *Studies on Hysteria* (1893–95). *SE* II.

Gallop, Jane. 'Keys to Dora'. In *In Dora's Case: Freud, Hysteria, Feminism*, 200–220. Edited by Charles Bernheimer and Claire Kahan. London: Virago, 1985.

Gitelson, Maxwell. 'Therapeutic Problems in the Analysis of the "Normal" Candidate'. *International Journal of Psychoanalysis* 35 (1954): 174–83.

Glover, Edward. 'Therapeutic Criteria of Psycho-Analysis'. *International Journal of Psychoanalysis* 35 (1954): 95–101.

Klein, Melanie. 'Some Theoretical Conclusions Regarding the Emotional Life of the Infant (1952)'. In Melanie Klein, *Envy and Gratitude and Other Works, 1946–1963*, 61–93. New York: Free Press, 1984.

——— 'On the Sense of Loneliness (1963)'. In Melanie Klein, *Envy and Gratitude and Other Works, 1946–1963*, 300–313. New York: Free Press, 1984.

Lacan, Jacques. *Feminine Sexuality: Jacques Lacan and the École Freudienne*. Edited by Juliet Mitchell and Jacqueline Rose, translated by Jacqueline Rose. New York: W.W. Norton, 1982.

——— *The Seminar of Jacques Lacan, Book II: The Ego in Freud's Theory and in the Technique of Psychoanalysis, 1954–1955*. Edited by Jacques-Alain Miller, translated by Sylvana Tomaselli. Cambridge: Cambridge University Press, 1988.

——— *The Seminar of Jacques Lacan, Book III: The Psychoses, 1955–1956*. Edited by Jacques-Alain Miller, translated by Russell Grigg. New York: W.W. Norton, 1997.

——— *The Seminar of Jacques Lacan, Book VII: The Ethics of Psychoanalysis, 1959–1960*. Edited by Jacques-Alain Miller, translated by Dennis Porter. New York: W.W. Norton, 1997.

——— *The Seminar of Jacques Lacan, Book X: Anxiety*. Edited by Jacques-Alain Miller, translated by Adrian Price. Cambridge: Polity, 2014.

——— *The Seminar of Jacques Lacan, Book XI: The Four Fundamental Concepts of Psychoanalysis*. Edited by Jacques-Alain Miller, translated by Alan Sheridan. New York: W.W. Norton, 1998.

——— *The Seminar of Jacques Lacan, Book XVII: The Other Side of Psychoanalysis*. Translated by Russell Grigg. New York: W.W. Norton, 2006.

——— *The Seminar of Jacques Lacan, Book XX: On Feminine Sexuality, the Limits of Love and Knowledge, Encore 1972–1973*. Edited by Jacques-Alain Miller, translated by Bruce Fink. New York: W.W. Norton, 1999.

——— 'Aggressivity in Psychoanalysis'. In Jacques Lacan, *Écrits: The First Complete Edition in English*, 82–101. Translated by Bruce Fink. New York: W.W. Norton, 2006.

——— *Écrits: The First Complete Edition in English*. Translated by Bruce Fink. New York: W.W. Norton, 2006.

——— 'The Direction of the Treatment and the Principles of Its Power'. In Jacques Lacan, *Écrits: The First Complete Edition in English*, 489–542. Translated by Bruce Fink. New York: W.W. Norton, 2006.

——— 'The Mirror Stage as Formative of the *I* Function as Revealed in Psychoanalytic Experience'. In Jacques Lacan, *Écrits: The First Complete Edition in English*, 75–81. Translated by Bruce Fink. New York: W.W. Norton, 2006.

——— 'Variations on the Standard Treatment'. In Jacques Lacan, *Écrits: The First*

Complete Edition in English, 269–302. Translated by Bruce Fink. New York: W.W. Norton, 2006.

——— *My Teaching*. Translated by David Macey. London: Verso, 2008.

Leclaire, Serge. *Psychoanalyzing: On the Order of the Unconscious and the Practice of the Letter*. Translated by Peggy Kamuf. Stanford, CA: Stanford University Press, 1998.

Lefort, Rosine, in collaboration with Robert Lefort. *Birth of the Other*. Translated by Marc Du Ry, Lindsay Watson and Leonardo Rodríguez. Chicago: University of Illinois Press, 1994.

Loewald, Hans W. 'On the Therapeutic Action of Psychoanalysis'. In Hans W. Loewald, *The Work of Hans Loewald: An Introduction and Commentary*, 16–59. Edited by Gerald I. Fogel. Lanham, MD: Jason Aronson, 1991.

Masson, Jeffrey Moussaieff, ed. and trans. *The Complete Letters of Sigmund Freud to Wilhelm Fliess*. Cambridge, MA: Harvard University Press, 1985.

Preciado, Paul B. *Testo Junkie: Sex, Drugs, and Biopolitics in the Pharmacopornographic Era*. Translated by Bruce Benderson. New York: Feminist Press, 2013.

——— *An Apartment on Uranus: Chronicles of the Crossing*. Translated by Charlotte Mandell. Pasadena, CA: Semiotext(e), 2019.

——— *Can the Monster Speak? Report to an Academy of Psychoanalysts*. Translated by Frank Wynne. Pasadena, CA: Semiotext(e), 2020.

Reich, Wilhelm. *Character Analysis*. Translated by Vincent R. Carfagno. New York: Farrar, Straus and Giroux, 1980.

Rieff, Philip. *Freud: The Mind of a Moralist*. Chicago, IL: University of Chicago Press, 1979.

Roudinesco, Élisabeth. *Jacques Lacan & Co.: A History of Psychoanalysis in France, 1925–1985*. Translated by Jeffrey Mehlman. Chicago, IL: University of Chicago Press, 1989.

Verhaeghe, Paul. *Does the Woman Exist? From Freud's Hysteric to Lacan's Feminine*. Translated by Marc Du Ry. London: Rebus Press, 1999.

Webster, Jamieson. *Conversion Disorder: Listening to the Body in Psychoanalysis*. New York: Columbia University Press, 2018.

Webster, Jamieson, Alison Gingeras and Paul B. Preciado. 'Pathologically Optimistic: An Interview with Paul Preciado'. *Gagosian Quarterly* (winter 2020). https://gagosian.com/quarterly/2020/12/04/interview-pathologically-optimistic-paul-b-preciado/.

West, Nathanael. *Miss Lonelyhearts*. New York: New Directions, n.d. [1946].

An unravelling of what you thought you wanted

A dream is only the cut between one day and another, forming
the passage of time that is one's lived life. Death is everywhere
around us. Drive life, unconscious life, exists on the surface.

'The essential point of the dream is not so much that it resuscitates
the past as that it announces the future. It foretells and announces the
moment in which the patient will finally reveal to the analyst the secret
[he or she] does not yet know, which is nevertheless the heaviest
burden of [his or her] present . . . the dream anticipates the moment of
freedom.' (Agamben 2009)

Civilisation requires a loss in instinctual life. Psychoanalysis will always
be asocial since it demands that the patient take back the libido that has
been extracted in the service of civilisation.

The cure, according to Freud, was simply sexual satisfaction, which he
placed on the side of reality. If Freud was radically inhibited in reality,
bereft of his desire, it is the work with these dreams, his self-analysis,
which enables him to push forward and to take up his desire beyond
the sticky and inhibiting grasp of his narcissistic wishes.

'Look at the direction the boats are facing in the harbour and you'll know which
direction the wind is blowing.' How come I never noticed them all facing the same
direction before? I suppose I assumed they were tied up that way. What little sense I
have for the movement of water.

If you look for help, all you will find is someone else looking for it; but
what you fear is, in fact, what they want.

*What have I done? You were so much more interesting before you started
talking to me. And then I think twice about everything: I was so much more
interesting before I became a psychoanalyst.*

Procrastination, Lacan points out, is a kind of anal relationship to time, by which omnipotence is retained through a refusal of time.

Desire is precisely a force that calls on you to make a decision.

Have you lived in conformity with the desire that is in you?

One book always sets up the next. I want to write about what it means to have a sexual body and the search for sensuality. I don't know exactly what that's going to look like, but I feel like we've forgotten about how wonderful and dangerous sexuality is, or the feeling of being sexed.

Freud's self-analysis is the model; his self-testing of everything.

The unconscious is a kind of hell. A world without forgetting. A world where everything can return and what is lost is never forgotten. Who has the courage?

Sheer symptomatic repetition in treatments, as many of us know, feels lethal, and we perk up as the work of analysis mutates this repetition into something else.

Neurosis has a disintegrating, almost mocking, effect on institutions: the paranoiac as philosopher, the hysteric as artist, the obsessional creates religion.

The Wolf Man, having too much money and too much secondary gain from his illness, cannot really pay, meaning he cannot make the sacrifice of his symptom in the name of his psychoanalysis. Money means nothing to him. By what means do we gain access to desire? With what do we pay?

We were never, and have never been, at home in pleasure.

Lack not love might actually be the important determining force, which propels us into an unknown future, not some ground known in advance.

That which we tend to ignore in our happy illusions and tight social constructions of identity and nation.

It is my feeling that this desire for 'neutrality' is still a desire, so what you end up showing is your fear, which is going to turn people off, or on, or whatever. But if you think you are simply acting 'neutral' or 'correct' without understanding it as a desire in itself, then you certainly can't analyse it for its failures.

What many don't know about the poet Paul Celan is that there was a prior suicide attempt before the one that took his life. He stabbed himself in the heart with a letter opener, and also tried to murder his wife, the artist Gisèle Celan-Lestrange. The heart for Celan is, of course, a poetic trope, diastolic and systolic, it beats the very off-rhythm of poetry. A mistake in reading poetry is to assume that it's not literal for the poets.

Life is a deferral on the way to death, there is no reality except for the reality of death. The present is so open, and that openness isn't easy to bear.

Any figure of mastery other than death will lead to a closure of the unconscious.

What kind of knowledge is knowledge of death and what death does to knowledge.

Nothing could be further from desire than the desire to have desire.

Ambiguity is always present, since the future outruns the speaking person in question, who is always 'outstripped'.

Can what is said and the act of saying join together in a great unity, with the force of revelation?

Jamieson Webster is a psychoanalyst in New York City. She is the author of *The Life and Death of Psychoanalysis* (Karnac, 2011) and *Conversion Disorder* (Columbia University Press, 2018); she also co-wrote, with Simon Critchley, *Stay, Illusion! The Hamlet Doctrine* (Pantheon, 2013). She contributes regularly to *Apology*, *Artforum*, *Spike Art Magazine* and the *New York Review of Books*.